Praise for *The EduProtocol Field Guide Social Studies Edition*

EduProtocols have been an absolute game changer in my classroom! My students have shifted from wondering why they need to know history to becoming the lead learners in an adventure through time! Jon and Marlena describe EduProtocols as being structured enough to be consistent, yet open-ended enough that students can be creative and have a choice in demonstrating their learning. With EduProtocols, my students are able to demonstrate essential executive functioning skills while learning from a variety of historical documents that produce outcomes even the teacher is excited about sharing! The *EduProtocol Field Guide Social Studies Edition* is a book that I wish I would have had during my teacher-prep program. Adam and Scott have created a go-to guide for all social studies teachers that will provide you with dynamic student-centered experiences that can apply to every classroom. I can't say enough about all I have learned from these two amazing educators and the impact this book will have on your classroom.

—**Dominic Helmstetter,** social studies teacher, Perrysburg High School

EduProtocols allow teachers to leverage two of the most powerful but underutilized resources in education—technology and students—to create impactful, transformative learning experiences for ALL. Eliminate packets, worksheets, long lectures, an overreliance on the textbook, and other joy-sucking activities, and replace them with EPs that combine content, skill development, SEL, and UDL all in one package! EPs allow teachers to "peacefully procrastinate" on lesson planning during those extra busy weeks, without compromising the quality of the lesson. EPs will help shift the narrative of the typical history/social studies classroom from one that is primarily lecture-based, with students memorizing "important" facts, dates, and people, to one that empowers them to develop modern skills, own their learning, and make relevant, real-world connections. Quite possibly the most significant component of EPs is their simplicity; they do not require "rockstar" teachers for effective implementation. Adam and Scott are two very "normal" guys who have helped change the landscape of modern social studies education with their brilliant work, and you can, too!

—**Robert Mayfield,** instructional coach and social studies teacher, Ripon High School

Looking for a dynamic way to capture the interest of your learners? These protocols are accessible to every student! They provide opportunities for meeting diverse needs while still analyzing, comparing, and evaluating content. Adam gives the tools you need to make your classes creative and memorable, giving the class agency in molding the outcome of the lessons.

—**MaryKay Thede,** social studies teacher, New Richmond Middle School

Adam and Scott are leaders in sharing their creative ideas on social media, selflessly advancing the ability for more students to experience DOING history in school. They have now created this resource for teachers looking for ways to implement EduProtocols with social studies at the center. In writing this book, they pull the curtains back to expose concrete ways to implement EduProtocols for historical thinking, setting students up to construct meaning about the past and present. Teachers using this book will find approachable ways to remix familiar and new EduProtocols to put their students in the driver's seat as historians. As a former eighth-grade social studies teacher of fifteen years, I wish I had this book earlier in my career. Now, as an instructional coach, I am excited to study it with others. Adam and Scott have created an invaluable and unique resource—an authentic book for social studies teacher *by* social studies teachers.

—**Jen Page,** curriculum, instruction, and assessment specialist, Buckeye Valley Local Schools

The EduProtocol Field Guide Social Studies Edition

Bring Your Teaching into Focus

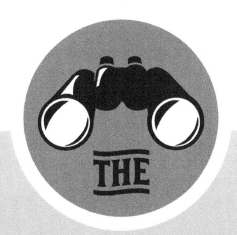

EduProtocol

FIELD GUIDE

SOCIAL STUDIES EDITION

— 13 —

Student-Centered Lesson Frames
for AP and College Prep

Dr. Scott M. Petri & Adam Moler

with Jon Corippo & Marlena Hebern

The EduProtocol Field Guide Social Studies Edition: 13 Student-Centered Lesson Frames for AP and College Prep
© 2022 Dr. Scott M. Petri, Adam Moler, Marlena Hebern, and Jon Corippo

This book is available at special discounts when purchased in quantity for educational purposes or for use as premiums, promotions, or fundraisers. For inquiries and details, contact the publisher at books@daveburgessconsulting.com.

Published by Dave Burgess Consulting, Inc.
San Diego, CA
DaveBurgessConsulting.com

Library of Congress Control Number: 2022942286
Paperback ISBN: 978-1-956306-31-6
Ebook ISBN: 978-1-956306-32-3

Cover and interior design by Liz Schreiter
Edited and produced by Reading List Editorial
ReadingListEditorial.com

Scott M. Petri would like to dedicate this book to Dr. Shawn Bird. Ten years ago, your calming and thoughtful advice prevented me from making the rash decision of leaving the education field. I am so grateful you took the time to mentor me and talk me off the ledge. Over the last decade, my work empowering students has been so rewarding and enriching. They exceed my expectations every year. You are a powerful role model, educational leader, and reminder that leadership, like teaching, is personal. We build one relationship at a time. We save lives one student at a time. Thank you for helping me overcome short-term setbacks and think big picture. I wish you the happiest and longest of education careers.

Adam Moler dedicates this book to his mom, Angel James, who is the ultimate teacher in life. Your examples of hard work and perseverance helped me reach this point.

Jon dedicates this book to his wife, Rhonda. Thank you for all you put up with.

Marlena dedicates this book to her husband, Walt. Without your patience and love, I'd probably still be using our little Apple IIe! Awww, the magic of color can change everything!

Contents

SECTION 1
Through the Social Studies Looking Glass

Chapter 1
How Scott and Adam Got Here

Scott's Story

The first teacher to introduce me to EduProtocols was Connie Mimura, whom I met after presenting at her district's Arcadia Innovation Summit. Connie asked if I would like to co-present with her on EduProtocols. She would provide middle school samples, and I could add some high school samples. I was not familiar with EduProtocols, but I didn't tell her that. I quickly bought the book and tried Cyber Sandwich with my students. Student engagement soared immediately. Students were taking about social studies content. I was sold. This started my EduProtocols journey.

Connie and I presented at three conferences the year we met. I didn't think our work was particularly brilliant, but other teachers kept tagging us on Twitter and sending us pictures of their student work. Since I've started working with EduProtocols, I've realized how much sharing and analyzing student work can help knock down the silos between subjects and move teams of teachers toward interdisciplinary collaboration. It can also bridge physical distances. I am frequently contacted by teachers who are working on high-level, project-based learning together despite the fact that they don't even teach at the same school. EduProtocols have brought them together.

Since joining the EduProtocols community, I have met many other teachers who are generous about sharing their classroom lessons and activities. I have learned that the #EduProtocol community is active and passionate. My social network and professional learning communities have grown, and I have connected with teachers outside of my subject and grade-level teams, like my coauthor, Adam Moler.

Adam is an eighth-grade US history teacher in Ohio. Like me, he is a #GirlDad, but he's also a vegetarian, so I had my doubts about working with him. For two years we've collaborated online and presented together at virtual professional development sessions. Eventually we met, in person, at Spring CUE, in March 2022. Adam is creative, enthusiastic, and always looking to bring more fun into his classroom. He has excellent taste in craft beer and can talk about IPAs for days.

In my own classroom, remixing and stacking EduProtocols has given my students rigorous daily workouts that challenge their Four Cs (creativity, collaboration, communication, and critical thinking skills). Plus, I spend less time planning and grading. I've witnessed how, with EduProtocols, my students do more creative and original deep thinking. They see patterns in their work and discuss them when in their collaborative sessions. As they become better communicators and analysts, they are able to make connections to other ideas and concepts. For example, when doing a Cyber Sandwich on the Bloody Sunday that sparked the Russian Revolution, my tenth-grade students made connections to the French Revolution, the Haitian Revolution, the civil rights movement, and the January 6 Capitol Insurrection. These were conversations happening between teenagers over Zoom. I was not directing them. I was eavesdropping on them, and what I heard made me feel like I should win one of those History Teacher of the Year awards.

With EduProtocols, Jon Corippo and Marlena Hebern have created a movement that benefits all teachers. When I first encountered EduProtocols, I thought they were a little pedestrian and maybe only suitable for elementary and middle school students. Then I started using them to help my Honors and AP students who were struggling with nonfiction. Instead of confusing my students with dozens of historical figures and references, I began frontloading retrieval practice with crowdsourced Iron Chefs. Armed with historical context, students understood more, which resulted in more positive reading experiences.

This book will showcase the familiar EduProtocols that have lent themselves particularly well to history and social studies instruction at all levels, and we'll show you exactly how to adapt them to different groups of learners and these subjects. We'll also introduce some new protocols such as Archetype Four Square, the Hero's Journey, Research, and Retell in Rhyme.

The success of the EduProtocol franchise comes from the simplicity of the protocols. The fact that they can be seamlessly integrated and understood by students ranging from K–12 makes them valuable tools for teachers. Use them, as advertised, to bring your teaching into focus, and I think you'll enjoy your EduProtocols journey as much as I have.

Adam's Story

Most of us have that one life-changing moment we never forget. My life-changing moment happened several years ago in my old classroom, Room 303. A student raised her hand and asked me, "Why are we doing these maps? I don't learn anything from them."

I didn't have an answer. I couldn't justify the worksheet that I had assigned.

At that moment, I realized the worksheets and the one-size-fits-all format I'd been using weren't working. As a result, I had every student get up and throw the maps away. This experience launched my search to find better tools for my seventh- and eighth-grade students and my teaching.

I found those tools a few years ago when I ordered *The Edu-Protocol Field Guide*. My classroom needed a jolt, and "student-centered" lessons grabbed my attention. When I received the book, I flipped through the pages searching for that something better. Searching for something creative. However, because I'm a social studies teacher, the language arts and math lessons didn't jump out at me. I wasn't sure it was what I was looking for, and I put the book aside until a couple of months later, in January 2018.

I decided to give EduProtocols another chance and rolled out an Iron Chef about Andrew Jackson for my eighth-grade social studies class. My Iron Chef looked engaging, was student-centered, and had great questions, embedded videos, and readings.

Major fail. The students focused on the process instead of the content. They were clearly overwhelmed.

I went too big, too fast, and posted my failure on Instagram. One day later, Jon Corippo commented on my post and helped me understand how to approach an Iron Chef for next time. (He truly is a #helpfulguy.) The one comment that stuck with me was, "Did you do a couple of nonacademic practice rounds first? The kids need a couple of reps to acclimate."

In addition to being a middle school social studies teacher, I'm also a tennis player and coach, so Jon's advice to use practice and repetition really resonated. This is how I taught tennis for many years. Why should classroom teaching be any different? Once my students got the hang of it through some practice and repetition with the lesson frames, the Iron Chef EduProtocol gave them the ability to create their own presentations. The Cyber Sandwich generated great discussions. 8*pARTS sparked creative discussions about historical photographs. Sketch and Tell helped me create more hands-on social studies lessons. Students have a choice through Play-Doh, Legos, or food to explain their learning.

Prior to my search for something better, when my student asked me why we were using blank maps, I didn't have a clue myself. With EduProtocols, I have a clear, consistent criteria for what and how I teach. I build every lesson around the Four Cs: critical thinking, creating, collaboration, and communicating learning. The EduProtocols support these, and that's my why for every lesson and my why for every day I teach.

EduProtocols are versatile and don't require fancy technology or overused apps. Transformative teaching comes down to asking the right questions, providing choice, and giving students a clear path to mastery. The EduProtocols provide all of these opportunities, whether a teacher opts to use technology or have students work on paper.

For the past four years, I have found success with mixing up how I implement EduProtocols in social studies. Most people who know me view me as a technology wizard, but I genuinely feel it's best to balance paper-based lessons with technology-based lessons. For example, I will run a Cyber Sandwich protocol on paper several times throughout the year. With paper, I notice students write thoughts in their own words. I've noticed students rereading the material and interacting with the text more often.

In this book you will find a variety of EduProtocols tailored toward middle and high school history students, including AP-level social studies courses. You will also find many student samples and instructional templates. All of these ideas can be easily implemented with computers or on paper. The choice is yours and depends on what's better for your students.

EduProtocols **are lesson frames into which you will insert your curriculum to teach more effectively and deliver more engaging content.** Each EduProtocol supports one of the Four Cs. (There are a few exceptions, like Fast and Curious.)

The Four Cs, identified by the Partnership for 21st Century Skills, are four skills that are considered essential for modern students, skills that successful adults use every day in and out of the workplace:

Collaboration: Using interpersonal and intrapersonal skills when working with peers.

Communication: Sharing one's work, research, and projects with other students and adults inside and outside the four walls of the classroom.

Critical Thinking: Analyzing problems, data, research, literature, or mathematics by solving real-world problems.

Creativity: Open-ended and choice-driven activities in which students have autonomy in the process and results so creativity can flourish.

We want to see students collaborating, creating, critically thinking, and communicating, and we want you to know that you can use the ideas presented here to enrich student engagement through the Four Cs and change your classroom!

We will challenge students to dig deeper while keeping the technology skill level for teachers fairly streamlined. Most protocols use Google Slides or PowerPoint as the foundation.

By their very nature, EduProtocol lesson frames are adaptive as the curriculum changes and students move from one topic to another in their studies. Once students have learned a particular lesson frame, the teacher is able to repeat that lesson frame again and again with a variety of content throughout the year. This allows for students to gain familiarity with a process that can be used repeatedly for learning throughout the year.

EduProtocols are suitable for students across the grade span, from kindergarten through adult learner, and allow the learner to engage with the Four Cs (collaboration, critical thinking, communication, and creativity) in a format that supports Universal Design for Learning (UDL). Not all of the protocols tap into all of the Four C skills, but most do at varying levels. You can find detailed information about the Four Cs in chapter 14, "The Four Cs Throwdown," in *The EduProtocol Field Guide, Book 1*.

EduProtocols Help Manage Cognitive Load

When students jump from one activity to the next, day in and day out, they lose their ability to focus on the content. Perpetually relearning tasks wears and tears on students. The EduProtocols allow students to learn one task and then apply it to a variety of content "lessons," thus maximizing their energy and focusing their effort on the content at hand.

You may have heard this described as the zone of proximal development (ZPD), developed by Lev Vygotsky in the 1930s. The ZPD describes a state of mind when a learner is working in the space between "cannot complete on my own" (frustration) and "can completely do on my own" (boredom). When students work in the space between cannot and can, they are challenged at just the right level and are most open to new learnings. Too much, too fast, and the learner shuts down. Too slow, and the learner does not pay close attention because they already know it all. Just right, and the learner excels.

By scaffolding learning with the EduProtocols, we allow the ZPD to become hyperfocused on the content instead of the lesson design. Students, regardless of age, feel enormously successful when they accomplish a lesson with little direction because they already know how. Managing the cognitive load, the ZPD of the student experience, is the magic dust of the EduProtocols that makes all the other goodness possible.

If you are trying to wrap your brain around this concept, think about the process of posting an image on Instagram. There are several specific steps to sharing an image:

- Find the perfect shot
- Snap the image
- Open the app
- Add the image to the app
- Adjust the color and use the editing options
- Write a caption and choose your hashtags
- Post the image and wait for your friends to see it and comment

Next time you find that perfect shot, you will repeat the same basic steps to post the image. Those steps remain the same, but the image and the circumstances for taking the perfect shot change each time you post. Imagine how frustrating it would be if the steps to post an image changed every time you opened the app.

Using Instagram feels complicated at first. It is a struggle to make just the right edits. However, with a little practice, the process becomes familiar, and you soon find that your concentration shifts to the art of framing the perfect composition with just the right lighting instead of on how to find the photo library in the app. When you look at someone's profile on Instagram, notice how the skillfulness of their photography has evolved since their earliest posts. Can you see the ZPD shift in the Instagram example? At first it was all about how to post, but later on it became about the artistry of taking a picture.

Students will do the same with EduProtocols, and once they grow into them, they will shift their focus from the logistics of the lesson procedures to the art and joy of actual learning, a key strategy when content difficulty increases at the upper levels of middle school, high school, and in AP work. With the slightly gamified approach of EduProtocols, students are often willing to tackle work beyond their initial abilities.

It takes most classes two to five repetitions of an EduProtocol to master it. The sweet spot is achieved when automaticity is reached, and a student's focus shifts from how to complete the process to mastering the content. When deploying EduProtocols in your classroom, you will feel this shift. Students will recognize the protocol by name and get right to work completing it.

The most successful teachers take time in the first weeks of school to update students on classroom procedures: where to get the paper, when to sharpen pencils, how to put away the laptops, and how to exit the classroom. Experienced teachers understand the importance of training students in the first days of school in face-to-face classrooms. This early training can give you a head start in deploying protocols with content. But if you are starting late in the year, or introducing a protocol midway through the year, simply take time to allow students to learn the process before diving into your content. Go slow to go fast. You will reap the benefits later on, and your time up front will pay off down the road.

How to Read This Book

You can read this book from cover to cover and enjoy insights and stories about the EduProtocols, but you can also opt to skip to a specific EduProtocol to try in your classroom. Near the end you'll find advice on "stacking," "smashing," and "racking and stacking" EduProtocols throughout your teaching day and extending units into EduProtocol sequences.

However you choose to read this book, use it to bridge the gap between subject matter and delivery with meaningful EduProtocols you create with your content. EduProtocols are formatted to get kids collaborating, creating, thinking critically, and communicating. And this book is formatted to help you start planning now.

Make notes in the space provided in the margins. We want this guide to be something you refer back to again and again. We hope you find it to be valuable.

We love to hear what teachers are doing and hope you'll share your progress, insights, and the lessons you create!

We love to hear what teachers are doing and hope you'll share your progress, insights, and the lessons you create!

Connect with us on Twitter:
- *@moler3031*
- *@scottmpetri*
- *@mhebern and*
- *@jcorippo*

Visit our website:
- *eduprotocols.com*

Visit the EduProtocols Social Studies site for templates and student examples.

SECTION 2

EduProtocols for Social Studies

Chapter 3
Fast and Curious EduProtocol

Shortly after finishing his third Quizizz of the week, covering the Magna Carta, a seventh-grade student said to Adam, "I used to cram in the morning the day of the test to get a good grade.** Then I would forget what I was tested on. This cycle would repeat for the next test. With the Fast and Curious repetitions, I can memorize the content. Learning is a muscle memory for me." This student's experience speaks to the effectiveness of the Fast and Curious EduProtocol in helping students commit to memory specific information they will need later on in a unit of study.

The class's first attempt at the Magna Carta quiz.

Why? Spaced (over time) practice is more effective than mass (cramming) practice. Most teachers with enough experience know this, but many students still think that cramming is a faster way of learning. On John Hattie's updated 2018 list of *252 Influences and Effect Sizes Related to Student Achievement*, spaced v. mass practice had an effect size of 0.60. Fast and Curious continually asks students to recall what they learned the day before, allowing mastery to happen over time.

THE MAGNA CARTA ☑ Edit
🕐 March 3rd 2021, 12:33 PM (5 months ago)

View quiz   Flashcards   Live Dashboard

92% Accuracy   8 Questions   13 Participant Attempts

The class's final attempt at the same quiz.

Description:

The easiest way to get started with EduProtocols is through a Fast and Curious. Take your social studies worksheet, packet, or vocabulary and convert it into a Quizizz. If you are learning about the causes of the Revolutionary War, for example, create 10–15 questions and run the protocol for the first five minutes of class.

Repetition is the key to building retention and learning. After administering a Fast and Curious quiz once with feedback, try to run the same quiz again during that same class period. Then repeat as necessary throughout the week. This is how the Fast and Curious EduProtocol can combat the forgetting curve.

Using Quizizz, Gimkit, or Blooket continuously and repeatedly throughout the week entails a simple shift in how you use technology to effectively track student progress. Students can own their learning and chart progress during the week. This visualization of averages is powerful in engaging students, building confidence, and driving them toward better. Focusing on class accomplishments rather than rewarding individual accomplishments keeps this protocol positive and supports the group's collective effort.

Academic Goals:

- Reinforce basic skills that are required for learning advanced skills.
- Help students retain information.
- Improve transfer of knowledge.
- Build confidence among your students.

Adam

If your Quizizz class average is super high on the first rep, review your questions. Maximize Fast and Curious by avoiding the "low-hanging fruit" types of questions.

Jon

Repetition is the key to locking terms into long-term memory. Also, people feel safe when they know they can get better. These are all keys to the success of the Fast and Curious EduProtocol. Make sure you look up the "forgetting curve" to learn more about this!

Teacher Big Ideas:

- This protocol helps to establish a routine to start off class and get students settled in.
- A lot of quiz platforms allow for quizzes to be taken live or set up as homework assignments for students who are absent.
- Students will work harder to raise the class score as a community is built around the achievement of all. Focus on the class score.

Prepare for the Activity:

Fast and Curious is an easy EduProtocol to set up through Quizizz, Gimkit, Blooket, or Quizlet Live. Many of these programs offer premade quizzes you can copy and reuse, or simply create your own quiz to fit your social studies content.

Instructions:

Step 1: Find or create a quiz using a program like Quizizz, Gimkit, or Blooket.

Step 2: Create 10–15 questions related to the content for the week.

Step 3: Consider starting with five questions and gradually adding new questions throughout the week.

Step 4: Start off class with your quiz and start a timer for five minutes.

Step 5: When the quiz concludes, or time is up, go through the most commonly missed questions and provide feedback immediately.

Step 6: Have students record their percentages daily using a provided template or spreadsheet, but keep a general focus on the class score.

Step 7: Pair Fast and Curious with a Frayer or another EduProtocol, and run the same quiz again at the end of class.

Marlena

Resist the urge to play again and again on the same day. (Yeah, it's that fun!) Remember, spaced practice is better for mastery over time!

Adam

When providing feedback for students on the commonly missed questions, ask them what they think the second-best answer would be, to help them understand why they missed the question(s).

Key Points to Remember:

- Create or find a quiz that's 10–15 questions to keep the flow moving.
- At the beginning of a lesson, do two reps of the quiz in one class period.
- Track the class score on the board. It's okay to have friendly competitions with other periods—even across subjects—but keep it light and fun. Everyone wins with EduProtocols!
- If crunched for time, assign the first rep as homework in a flipped classroom adaptation. Students complete the first rep at home, then review the vocabulary in class, and then immediately take the quiz again in class in an attempt to beat their own score.

ELL Tips:

Providing feedback after retrieval practice improves student metacognition. Look into using "exam wrappers" as described by Carnegie Mellon University's Eberly Center (cmu.edu/teaching/designteach/teach/examwrappers) that ask students how they prepared for an exam, specifically which study strategies they used and which they thought were most helpful. Dr. Pooja K. Agarwal suggests that allowing EL students to retake formative assessments frequently builds their confidence and vocabulary.

If students are researching historical figures, use a Google Sheet Quizizz template, give your students editing rights, and have them each contribute a question. With coaching and time, their questions will get better and better. Asking them to generate thirty-six questions for retrieval practice guarantees they will pay attention to all the student presentations. Plus, these can be converted into a Quizizz for reinforcement of content and concepts.

Scott

Having your students generate test questions from their individual work also improves retention.

Adapting for AP:

Author Annie Murphy Paul (@anniemurphypaul) has written extensively on the benefits of retrieval practice. In her *Scientific American* article "Researchers Find That Frequent Tests Can Boost Learning," Paul informs us that "every time a student calls up knowledge from memory, that memory changes. Its mental representation becomes stronger, more stable and more accessible." Fast and Curious can be used with AP History content to reduce anxiety before the AP exam. Simply borrow the released test questions from AP Central, paste them into Quizizz or Kahoot, and give your students daily retrieval practice on the AP content you have been teaching.

Chapter 4
Thin Slides EduProtocol

Thin Slides is a metacognition strategy to get students to reflect on what they already know about historical content and to assess what they want to know. Before our class's Renaissance meet and greet, students had three minutes to create one slide with one picture about an important fact related to the Renaissance influencer they'd chosen to study. At the end of three minutes, it was presentation time. Each student gave a quick five-second presentation from their desk as we zipped through the slides. The result of this low-prep, high-return activity? Better, more confident discussions among students.

The biggest takeaway from Thin Slides: getting the most out of student learning doesn't need to involve lots of time and elaborate presentations. Simple is sometimes better. To get the most out of a Socratic seminar, discussion, or research lesson, activate student thinking with Thin Slides.

Description:

With the Thin Slides EduProtocol, each student creates a single slide, which becomes part of a larger class slide deck. Give the students a key concept such as a theme, question, or word to explore for five minutes. In this example, we asked the question, "How did your Renaissance influencer change the world?" Students create a slide with one word and one image in five minutes. When the timer goes off, change the share settings on the Google Slide deck,

Scott

I used Thin Slides all through pandemic learning to make sure I heard from every student, every day. The prompts can be simple, like "What did you learn today?" Or you can stack them so that students can document the five biggest points from a *15 Minute History* lecture.

and have each student give a quick five-second presentation from their desk. Speed and student input is the key to Thin Slides.

Academic Goals:

- Achieve quick historical thinking and concept development.
- Develop creativity and visual communication.
- Develop speaking and listening skills among students.

Teacher Big Ideas:

- A great pre- or post-instruction strategy.
- Speed keeps the students engaged. Five-second presentations aren't as intimidating as one- or two-minute presentations.
- Thin Slides help build skills for other EduProtocols such as the Cyber Sandwich or Iron Chef.

Prepare for the Activity:

Determine your key concept. For example, Renaissance influencers, using the word *rights* paired with a Constitution lesson, or exploring GRAPES (Geography, Religion, Achievements, Politics, Economics, Social Structure) related to countries, colonies, or civilizations.

Create a shareable slide deck with some supports such as a term or some minimal details, or share blank slides and see what the students create.

Instructions:

Step 1: Model the format of Thin Slides so students know what they are doing. Many students are used to creating slides with too much information.

Step 2: Share a slide deck with students along with your prompt.

Step 3: Set a five-minute timer for students to explore and create their slide.

Adam

Having one word per slide ensures students aren't reading word for word from their slide during presentations. They are creating their own learning and thinking.

Marlena

To keep presentations moving along and short, try limiting students to one word per slide. That's a tangible limit students understand.

Adam

Keep things moving! Enforce the three- to five-minute timer for slide design and five-second limit for presentations. Have the students present from their seats.

Step 4: Click through the slides and have each student give a five-second presentation.

Key Points to Remember:

- Enforce the time. Speed creates engagement.
- Keep this activity simple.
- Thin Slides can help create better discussions with Socratic seminars and debates.
- This can be useful for exit tickets and reviews at the end of a lesson.

ELL Tips:

Thin Slides is an excellent EduProtocol for ELL students due to the limited writing. Allow think time before asking ELL students to speak about their sides.

Providing images for ELL students and having them explain their connections to historical details or other facts or concepts is an innovative way to use Thin Slides to support language acquisition. The teacher finds the image, and the student finds the one-word connection and explains it. Or reverse the process. Provide the word, and have the student find the image!

Adapting for AP:

Thin Slides can be used to help students practice with content-specific vocabulary words. Simply provide a list of words that ask students to identify and explain an historical concept, development, or process.

Students can then use the deck to practice learning about the current topic or concepts.

Adam

Teach students to do a Google image search using the explore button in Google Slides for photos that are available for commercial use or are copyright free.

Check out Scott's Thin Slide lesson!

Modifications:

Prepare for an Exam

Ask students to think about an upcoming exam and what is important for them to remember. Allow just five seconds for sharing, popcorning around the room until everyone has had a turn. As students present their slides, a review of the content will naturally unfold. Use your Ryan Seacrest voice to add or redirect students during this process so that the most important information is covered. Encourage students to take notes on a study guide to direct their focus when they leave to study on their own.

Exit Ticket

Take the last ten minutes of class two to three times a week and ask, "What did you learn today?" Students get three to five minutes to prepare and five seconds to present. This is a metacognition strategy to have students process their learning and hear five-second sound bites of peer learning as well. We've provided some examples that came from a lesson on the development of the women's suffrage movement. Students included one word, one picture, and an explanation for their learning. Students presented their slides from their desks in five seconds or less. This is great for developing public speaking and writing skills.

Suffragette

The name "Suffragette" was used in England to make fun of woman who wanted suffrage. It was used to make them look childish, but the women decided to not let the men have the power and so they decided to use it as their newspaper name. This is how the suffragists in England became suffragettes.

Coverture

Coverture is the legal statement that a married woman is owned by her husband. Her husband can do whatever he wants with her and any money she makes belongs to him.

Exit ticket Thin Slides.

Writing Prompts

Thin Slides are a great tool to help students write claims for their writing. In one particular lesson, we wanted to help students learn how to write a simple claim without using a pronoun. To help with writing claims, students watched a Doritos commercial that contained a cat who disappeared. Then students used the Thin Slide EduProtocol to write one word and used one image on their slide to answer a fun prompt: "What happened to the cat?" In the speaker notes, they wrote a claim about the question using their word from the slide. At the end of five minutes, students read their claims. This was a powerful lesson because students heard each other's claims, and it allowed the teacher to give feedback in real-time. This simple lesson helped set up students to write claims for our lesson's essential question: "What led most to the advancement of Islam: innovation, trade, or conflict?" Students used their claims to construct a paragraph with evidence and reasoning.

Study Guide

In the study guide variation, every student gets assigned a word, and the slide deck is shared with them. Students include their word, paraphrase the definition, and insert a picture. Give students five minutes of creation time to keep the flow moving. Then, the following day, shuffle all the kids and ask them to redo somebody else's slide. Students will add new pictures and new definitions for the same words. Allow the student who created the original version of the slide to give input on the upgraded slide to create a collaborative piece. And then, on day three, repeat again. Three solid reps before the test, and almost no prep for the teacher.

Historical Image as a Prompt

Use an historical image as a prompt for a Thin Slide. Ask students to reflect on the image and then create a Thin Slide in response to a prompt. For example, you might use the historical photo of Lyndon B. Johnson with Jacqueline Kennedy still in her blood-soaked dress by his side as he takes the presidential oath on *Air Force One*. The photo was taken just two hours after John F. Kennedy was assassinated in Dallas on November 22, 1963. Direct students with a prompt such as "What does this image make you feel?" or "What do you think the country was experiencing at this moment?"

Scott

Stacking Thin Slides can be a great way to help students build an Ignite Talk. Remember students need to be coached to make the image the focus of the slide and teach them how to use Word Art to make their clue pop.

Chapter 5
8 p*ARTS: Document-Based Questions EduProtocol

Scott

Amanda Sandoval (@historysandoval) developed an 8 p*ARTS for students viewing TED-Ed videos to record their knowledge. I like to use the website rarehistoricalphotos.com because it gives students context for a photo prior to using 8p*ARTS to analyze it.

Scan the QR code for Amanda Sandoval's template.

Apopular but ineffective strategy used in social studies classrooms to get students to slow down and think about historical images is "I See, I Think, I Wonder." A picture is projected, and students make a three-columned chart labeled, "I See, I Think, I Wonder." Students fill out the "I See" column with some observations and leave the next two columns blank. This, in a typical classroom, would be followed by some lackluster discussion, and then the class would move on to the main lesson. We've observed that students don't engage deeply with the image or apply their critical thinking skills when using this strategy, which is why, once we discovered it, 8 p*ARTS quickly became our go-to EduProtocol to analyze historical images and to develop creative writing skills.

Description:

The 8 p*ARTS EduProtocol invites students to think differently about image analysis, as the framework asks students to work with parts of speech while developing curiosity about the images. 8 p*ARTS is useful at the start of a lesson or can be used throughout a unit. Find interesting historical images, paintings, political cartoons, or even videos to use for analysis. Have students work individually or partnered up for discussion.

Academic Goals:

- Provide a catalyst for deeper understanding.
- Allow students to be their own guides in learning.
- Develop vocabulary centered around an image.

Teacher Big Ideas:

The 8 p*ARTS EduProtocol works well when beginning a new lesson. However, historical image analysis works best when the process is repeated multiple times during a unit. It works extremely well with interesting photos. For example, when starting off the westward expansion unit, use the painting entitled, *American Progress*, by John Gast. This image provides for a powerful introduction because there is a lot to observe; it tells a story. It contains a large floating angel, prospectors, covered wagons, and symbolism throughout. This iconic painting generates curiosity and interest. Ask students to write down five questions they have about the image.

Marlena

Wonder where the name 8 p*ARTS came from? 8 p*ARTS was designed for the 8 p*ARTS of speech, but it works beautifully as a catalyst for historical image analysis as well!

Three Word Title		
Heading	Somewhere	new

Verbs	Adverbs	Summarize		Nouns	Adjectives
flying	Far	This painting takes place in 1872. It looks as if they are moving and/or traveling somewhere. There are people with horses and wagons full of their belongings. They desperately look like they want the rough traveling on foot to be over. They are just walking along a dirt road next to big fields of animals and other people. Some people are also riding on the horses.		Horses	tough
walking	Slowly			Wagon	uncomfortable
riding	Roughly			Wild animals	desperately

Time Period		Conjunctions
1872		And, yet
Setting		Pronouns
Fields and dirt roads		They, her, him.

Simile (comparing 2 things using 'like' or 'as')
The horses are probably as tired as a bear in hibernation.

8 p*ARTS used with the painting *American Progress*, by John Gast.

Adam

I love how 8 p*ARTS gets students to make simple observations with historical photographs and deeply think of their observations in terms of language arts skills: nouns, adjectives, verbs, and adverbs. Plus, students are using historical thinking skills such as sourcing, contextualizing, and close reading.

Jon

When we use 8 p*ARTS in language arts, we gain a lot of time because of the workflow of teaching kids multiple skills in a single setting. Classically, language arts will do one part of speech per week for eight weeks, which equates to a quarter. With 8 p*ARTS, we do all eight parts of speech at one time. If we do this activity for twenty to twenty-five days, the students will have seen each part of speech for twenty-five days instead of just five days. It's dramatically more repetitions for the kids, with less work for teachers. You can apply this same strategy to historical image analysis!

Prepare for the Activity:

Step 1: Create a template in a slide program or drawing program such as Google Drawings.

Step 2: Find interesting historical images such as the unfinished painting *Treaty of Paris*, by Benjamin West, from 1783, or the painting *American Progress*, by John Gast. These paintings can help students create descriptive language, lead to many questions, and create curiosity.

Instructions:

Step 1: Share the protocol with students using slides or a Google Drawing or Jamboard.

Step 2: Students work in pairs or individually as they analyze an interesting historical image, painting, or political cartoon, searching for symbolism and nouns.

Step 3: Students give the historical image a three-word title.

Step 4: Students try to contextualize the image and think of the time period and setting.

Step 5: Students think of "I wonder" questions.

Step 6: Students use their found words, three-word phrases, contextualizing, and questions to write a descriptive paragraph analyzing the image and placing it in historical context.

Step 7: Use the template over and over again on a regular basis. Just insert a new image!

Step 8: As momentum toward mastery is gained, transition to independent work.

Key Points to Remember

- When introducing the protocol, utilize the 8 p*ARTS daily with goofy, funny images so students can focus on the process.

- As students become familiar with the process, start to use images and paintings that have a story to tell.

- This one protocol replaces many worksheets throughout the entire school year.
- This protocol results in a reduced workload for teachers as you have a great open-ended graphic organizer to use for writing.
- Grading is done immediately as the teacher circulates the room and provides assistance as students work.
- As mastery is gained, go for fluency and speed.

ELL Tips:

8 p*ARTS is a valuable tool for ELL students because it is already light on the writing. Allow scaffolds that ELL students typically use in class such as dictionaries, etc. Working in groups to generate the list of words together before beginning writing is also helpful.

Adapting for AP:

In an AP-level high school course, use 8 p*ARTS as a format for students to review eras in world or US history that will be covered by the Advanced Placement test. The template is easy for students to fill out and can be assigned individually or as a whole-class slideshow for studying purposes. Simply create a list of key terms, people, and events from a particular unit of study and let your students crowdsource the most important facts.

For college prep classes, use the 8 p*ARTS EduProtocol to have students review and summarize each other's work on larger projects. During a project-based learning (PBL) unit, Scott's tenth-grade world history students created over forty children's books on Mexican Revolution political leaders. Students then read each other's books. This allowed the creators of the books to get valuable feedback (a .70 Hattie effect size) from their peers, but more importantly it helped students improve with evaluation and reflection (an even bigger .75 Hattie effect size). Not to mention, it ensured that students read and learned about multiple leaders from the revolution. Using 8 p*ARTS made sure that each book got a

Check out student samples at eduprotocols.com

response from an authentic audience member, a crucial but frequently overlooked component of PBL.

Modifications:

8 p*ARTS is easy to modify based on the image or lesson being used. A simple modification of the subheadings can make 8 p*ARTS useful and effective for social studies.

- Students look for symbolism with nouns for a political cartoon or painting instead of describing the nouns with adjectives.
- Students can create "I wonder" statements or questions. This an effective tool with an inquiry-based unit.
- Students can think about the audience and purpose of a political cartoon or painting.

Scott

World history teacher Kathryn Greene (@MsGreeneEdu) uses 8 p*ARTS so that students can write historical summaries of frequently tested AP concepts like imperialism.

From this memorable experience, I learned many things. One of them was how to paraphrase significantly. I figured out how to use the info given and to transform it into something even better. My first attempt wasn't perfect, but then after listening to my other classmates' first attempt, I knew how to improve my writing to make it truly magnificent. When it was complete, I was proud of all the hard work I had put into this small assignment. I had learned many things doing this tiny writing assignment and will always use these valuable lessons whenever I paraphrase.

—Fourth-grade student in Mrs. Amy Terrell's class after completing a ParaFLY

See how Scott introduces ParaFLY.

Paraphrasing helps build important literacy skills that are used in middle and high school social studies. It helps students use repeated reading, build note-taking skills, and sharpen vocabulary usage as they decide how to describe the original text. What once seemed like a daunting task for most students now becomes easier with ParaFLY! This EduProtocol was named for the idea that students will paraphrase on the fly.

Description:

In ParaFLY, students use a complex reading task such as a primary source or an informational text to paraphrase. The teacher guides the students one paragraph at a time, having them reword

Jon

I modified the flow of the Random Emoji Power Paragraph when I realized my 2020 sixth-grade class was not only struggling with paraphrasing, they were actually afraid of the idea of paraphrasing. We needed a break-through, and ParaFLY was born.

important components of the sentences. Students are challenged to adjust the sentence structure while preserving the meaning of the text.

As a bonus, ParaFLY ensures students are grappling with high-level, text-based content in a very complete manner, like what you'd want them to accomplish by annotating, but with even higher levels of success and with a high degree of control for the teacher.

Academic Goals:

- Paraphrase without relying heavily on the original words of the author, demonstrating a true understanding of the text.
- Practice antiplagiarism skills by altering the original words and structure but providing credit to the original author.

Teacher Big Ideas:

- Teach students to use Rewordify.com or the Hemingway-App.com so that they don't have to do all the heavy lifting.
- Most Google Books offer the introduction or prologue for free. Ask your students to paraphrase challenging texts that are 5–8 pages in length and have 4–7 important or main ideas.

Prepare for the Activity:

To prepare for a ParaFLY, create an open-ended question with Socrative, Quizizz, or Mentimeter, or share a slides program so that students can access. Using one of these options will allow you to see the paraphrasing develop so you can offer immediate feedback in real time. Share only one paragraph of a primary source or informational text at a time, so the reading and paraphrasing task isn't overwhelming for students.

Scott

Sometimes I have students do a single ParaFLY in a whole-class deck, and other times I stack ParaFLY so that students go deeper and complete 3–5 slides on their own to demonstrate their comprehension of a text.

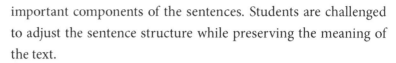

Marlena

Paraphrasing is important as it shows that the reader internalizes the content enough to express it in their own words.

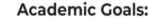

Adam

Rewordify works great with middle school students because it gives them a selection of words to choose from to understand passages within a difficult text.

Jon

I really like Socrative for ParaFLY, because I can do a short-answer quiz as fast as lightning, and when I hit "Start Vote," the kids can see each other's writing immediately.

Instructions:

Step 1: As always, start with some fun content first, such as the history of hamburgers or tacos. These first rounds of fun practice are key to all students mastering the ParaFLY skill-set.

Step 2: Share one paragraph of a primary source or informational text with students. This is the key to keeping it moving.

Step 3: Have students use a program such as Socrative or Quizizz, or even a shared slide deck for paraphrasing.

Step 4: Monitor student paraphrasing and provide feedback in real time.

Step 5: Repeat for 2–3 more paragraphs, sharing one paragraph at a time.

Note: As students gain paraphrasing skills, allow them to add one complete sentence from the text with "as mentioned in the article" or with a parenthetical citation, for example (Moler, 2021).

Step 6: Have students summarize what they learned today. Now the gloves are off—they can be artists.

Key Points to Remember:

- Introduce paraphrasing with a fun, less stressful reading.
- Think aloud with students to model the process.
- Only show the part of the document the students are paraphrasing, one paragraph at a time.

ELL Tips:

It may be helpful to work through samples together with English language learners so that students can see how we are rearraigning existing words and adding new words and synonyms to recreate the meaning in our own words.

Check out Scott's ParaFLY example on the Armenian Genocide.

Use a program such as Socrative so students can see the paraphrasing examples in real time. These examples and timely feedback are essential for ELLs to get the most out of paraphrasing. You can also provide your ELLs a list of vocabulary from the reading, or sentence starters, to help with paraphrasing.

Adapting for AP:

Using the ParaFLY EduProtocol makes it easier for teachers to focus on the historical thinking skills of sourcing and situating. Teachers provide excerpts from documents or speeches, and students practice identifying and explaining the source's point of view, purpose, historical situation, and/or audience. Teachers can also ask students to explain any limitations to the use of a source.

Modifications:

Jigsaw with ParaFLY

Use ParaFLY to facilitate jigsawing through an important speech. Give students sections of the speech, allow them to listen to an audio version of the speech or view the video (if available), or access a transcript and have them paraphrase the author's point of view.

Scott

I have also modified the ParaFLY protocol to help students practice explaining visual evidence. After providing one or two good examples, I turn them loose on a photo archive with hundreds of photos.

Chapter 7
Game of Quotes EduProtocol

Introduction:

The bell rings to end lunch, and the next period begins with sustained silent reading (SSR). Two students need to go to the library for a book, three students forgot a book, and four refuse to read. It's no fun being the SSR police. However, the Game of Quotes EduProtocol comes in for the rescue. The world-famous and now (sadly) retired ELA teacher-extraordinaire Heather Marshall developed this EduProtocol adapted from a game called Bring Your Own Book by GameWright (bringyourownbook.com). The game asks students to find a quote that responds to a borrowed phrase or creative prompt. The idea behind the game is that as students play, they get their peers interested in reading their book. Scott has used it differently because his high school students all read the same book. He blends historical fiction and nonfiction using titles like *Patriots from the Barrio*, *The Things They Carried*, and *Things Fall Apart*. Sometimes it is hard to get students to tell the difference between these two text types. Game of Quotes helps them dive into the text in front of them.

Description:

This game can also be adapted to help students practice and improve their historical thinking skills. Depending on the culture of your school, try using the College Board (AP) definitions, the Stanford History Education Group (SHEG) definitions, or the definitions from the American Historical Association (AHA). Since Scott's school is an AP Capstone school, he uses the nine historical thinking skills that the College Board has defined.

1. Analyzing evidence: content and sourcing
2. Interpretation

3. Comparison
4. Contextualization
5. Synthesis
6. Causation
7. Patterns of continuity and change over time
8. Periodization
9. Argumentation

SHEG defines four historical thinking skills and is a better choice for middle school students and high school underclassmen.

1. Sourcing
2. Contextualizing
3. Corroborating sources
4. Close reading

The AHA has the most complex definitions for its historical thinking skills.

1. Chronological thinking
2. Historical comprehension
3. Historical analysis and interpretation
4. Historical research skills
5. Historical issues: analysis and decision-making

These have been developed for college-level history classes.

Academic Goals:

- To help students connect to the text.
- To find textual evidence quickly.
- To improve recall of read material.

Teacher Big Ideas:

- Level questions by tying in literary devices or the AP, SHEG, or AHA definitions.
- Reinforce independent reading.

Marlena

Layering EduProtocols with academic goals such as the history definitions will develop strategic thinkers. And strategic thinkers will be successful leaders in a myriad of careers!

- Silent reading alone has little instructional value, so balance appropriately within your overall curriculum.

Prepare for the Activity:

If your students are unfamiliar with the definitions, consider front-loading students with a ParaFLY EduProtocol that invites them to rewrite the historical thinking skills in their own words. This will help you as a teacher because it will reveal their misconceptions. Curate some examples in advance, and be prepared to model them extensively.

Instructions:

Step 1: Students read quietly for eight to ten minutes.

Step 2: After the eight to ten minutes of reading, reveal the prompt for round one.

Step 3: The students flip through the pages of their books, looking for a good response to the prompt. Once a student says, "Got it!" the rest of the class has two minutes to lock in their answer.

Step 4: Students share their responses in table groups and vote on a winner. The table group winners share their answers one by one. It's okay not to vote on a winner or to allow students to share the best response from each table group.

Key Points to Remember:

- Have fun but go deeper into the standards or themes.
- Finding prompts in their books will reinforce learning goals.
- Students will want to flag potential quotes. Say yes!

ELL Tips:

ELL students will struggle with the complex vocabulary in nonfiction. Consider adding scaffolds such as Listenwise stories on the same topic, or use picture books that cover the same content. More advanced ELL students will be able to use Rewordify.com to better understand unfamiliar vocabulary words.

Adapting for AP:

For advanced players of the Game of Quotes, consider having students group their quotes into the four categories articulated by the College Board:

1. Analyzing historical sources and evidence
2. Making historical connections
3. Chronological reasoning
4. Creating and supporting an historical argument

Every AP exam question assesses one or more of these nine historical thinking skills and four thematic approaches. Being able to help students meet proficiency expectations dramatically helps their performance on the end-of-course exam.

Modifications:

If you do not have class sets of books or time within your pacing plan to have students read books, consider using longer excerpts. Scott uses one on the blinding of Sgt. Isaac Woodard. Readings of this size give students multiple opportunities to practice identifying historical thinking skills. Although it is easy to start asking them to identify text that showcases one skill at a time, after a few reps you can ask them to color code text that shows off the author's periodization, contextualization, and interpretation, and eventually they will be able to highlight all nine skills.

Check out student samples at eduprotocols.com

A **paradox in teaching high school is that text complexity goes up, but actual reading instruction goes down.** Many social studies teachers feel confident in their content instruction, but less so with their literacy strategies. These teachers often feel that more practice with reading is enough to make students proficient readers. It isn't. Students need purpose in their reading. They also need frequent and fast feedback on what they have read and understood. Enter the Cyber Sandwich—one of our favorite EduProtocols for getting students to dive into a complex reading assignment. The magic formula in Cyber Sandwich is the student discussion, because one student can have a completely different understanding of what was read than another. We have enjoyed adding layers of complexity to our Cyber Sandwich assignments over the years by featuring different readings and multiple forms of media, and by challenging students to explain the textual evidence they choose to include in their final paragraphs

Jon

Besides getting reading, writing, and collaboration jump-started, Cyber Sandwich lesson prep is usually less than ten minutes per lesson—lightning fast!.

Description:

Cyber Sandwich is a quick, ten-minute, digital think-pair-share activity that has been modified to a read-discuss/record-write format. The writing component creates accountability for the discussion; this is missing from a traditional think-pair-share.

There are two ways that Cyber Sandwich may be deployed:

a.) Both students read the same article and discuss their findings. (Better to begin with)

b.) Students read different articles and compare and contrast their findings. (More advanced version)

Start with Cyber Sandwich the traditional way: two students read one article, compare and contrast their notes in a discussion, and then, after considering what their peer's perspective brought up, they write individual paragraphs to demonstrate their understanding.

Once students have mastered this, try mixing it up by giving them two articles, preferably with different or conflicting information. This lends to more complex conversations and often results in significantly different paragraphs in the final step. Once that curveball does not fluster them anymore, group students into threesomes and foursomes and challenge them to develop an opinion or point of view based on their discussions.

Next, students spend five to ten minutes discussing their findings. The "compare and contrast" focus of the assignment centers their attention on which features are unique to each religion and what features they all have in common. After this, students have about ten minutes to write one paragraph about all three religions.

Pace this activity to allow for ten minutes to read, five minutes to discuss, and ten minutes to write. The quickness of the pacing avoids what Jon calls "The Suck," also known as Parkinson's law, where work expands so as to fill the time available for its completion. Regardless, whether one is idle or busy, the amount of work to be completed will take as long as the time allotted. In the trenches of K–12 classrooms, this means that students will take the entire amount of time given by the teacher to complete the task, whether they are given ten minutes or the whole class period. Therefore, if you need to tweak the time allotted, we recommend either shortening the reading, modifying the writing time with a Flipgrid reflection, moving the writing to homework, or skipping it altogether. The discussion is where the cognitive heavy lifting occurs.

Academic Goals:

Cyber Sandwich is a particularly cogent social studies EduProtocol, as it scaffolds and promotes student synthesis of readings. Synthesis is so much more than summarizing a text. It asks a reader to add their own original thinking, based on their life experiences, political opinions, and multiple interpretations to form new ideas.

Teacher Big Ideas:

In history, writing a synthesis can help students develop a deeper understanding, a new understanding, or a changed understanding, which causes them to think differently as a result of the text. All of these result in an increase in knowledge for the reader. Synthesis remixes ideas from across multiple texts and disciplines and from varied points of view to become innovative thinking or new understandings. In one Cyber Sandwich Scott did with his class, students were asked to select one person to be nominated for an award for saving Jewish people during the Holocaust. (This was a purely semantic assignment, as all four people shown have already been given this award by the Anti-Defamation League.) In this example, students argued among themselves over who deserved the award. Many students wound up changing their mind after hearing what one of their peers had to say about their person's heroic actions.

Jon
You can use ANY note-taking strategy for Cyber Sandwich—Notice and Note, AVID's WICOR, Milestones—they all work!

Prepare for the Activity:

Step 1: Select your text(s) and goals. Do you want the students to summarize and gain information about an historical person, place, or event? OR do you want your students to synthesize and become experts on a person, place, or event?

Step 2: Prepare the text students will be reading. Gather a link, article, website, or textbook section. The reading(s) should be no longer than a page and a half for a ten-minute read. Decide if you want to give students the reading in digital or print form.

Check out Scott's students' Courage to Care award sample.

Adam

You can find many free templates at eduprotocols.com or search #eduprotocols on Twitter.

Step 3: Identify struggling or EL students who may benefit from prereading the article beforehand. Prepare a copy for them.

Step 4: Prepare a five-slide deck with the following slides:

- Two note-taking slides (partner 1 notes, partner 2 notes)
- One slide divided into three parts (partner 1 notes, partner 2 notes, our common notes)
- Two slides for summary writing (partner 1 summary, partner 2 summary)

Instructions:

Step 1: One student will share the Cyber Sandwich slide deck with a partner.

Step 2: Students spend ten minutes reading a text individually while taking notes on a slide.

Step 3: Students spend the next ten minutes moving the content of their note-taking slide to a Venn diagram slide and discuss their findings with their partner. Through this discussion, students complete the final space in the Venn diagram, where they indicate what they both noticed in the reading.

Step 4: Using the note-taking sides for both partners and the Venn diagram notes as resources, each student spends a final ten minutes writing his or her own paragraph summarizing the information gathered on the slides. Alternately, students may summarize their findings in Flipgrid or via screencast.

Key Points to Remember:

Adjust the rigor of a Cyber Sandwich by either reducing the amount of reading time or increasing the text complexity. Student discussion time and writing time should remain constant. The goal of Cyber Sandwich is to increase reading reps and develop comprehension. Consider including a checklist of elements to facilitate self-review of work. Preparing "success charts" takes very little time and will help to dramatically improve the quality of feedback when grading student writing.

Label sources so that students can include a parenthetical (in-text) citation. Citing sources is a big deal in college-level writing, so both history and English teachers focus on teaching it at most schools.

Students can create paragraphs that include differences, similarities, and unique conclusions and then build these into larger and more complex writing assignments.

ELL Tips:

Sentence starters and vocabulary scaffolds are a great way to support ELL students. On the summary slide, provide a link to a list of potential sentence starters that are great for writing summaries. Here are a few examples:

- The main idea of the reading is . . .
- Today I learned . . .
- The big idea from _____ is . . .

Before diving into a Cyber Sandwich reading, have students skim for unknown vocabulary words. Use a word cloud program or graffiti board to have students share unknown words. Follow this up with a discussion of the vocabulary, or pair with another EduProtocol such as a Frayer or Sketch and Tell.

Adapting for Middle School: Main Idea Note-Taking Strategy

A modification for middle school students involves adding the main idea note-taking strategy. This strategy is a perfect fit with any Cyber Sandwich. On the notes slide, add a table that includes the following: turn the title into a question, who, what, when, where, how, and main idea titles. With this strategy, student 1 will read the text first as student 2 listens and takes notes. Then student

Marlena

Directing the focus of the Cyber Sandwich or any EduProtocol through specific prompts is a powerful way to target specific learning goals. Edu-Protocols are easily adaptable!

Scott

The Cyber Sandwich is one of the most flexible EduProtocols for social studies teachers. In high school, I use it to have students understand nuances in multiple texts, compare social studies concepts, and evaluate events and speeches. Integrate it into your classroom instruction as often and as creatively as possible.

2 reads as student 1 takes notes. The students will compare their notes and then summarize what they learned.

Adapting for Middle School: One Reading Source

When first using Cyber Sandwich, Adam tried asking his middle school students to compare two different texts, with mixed results. Scott and Jon helped Adam realize that he could have students read the same text or watch the same video, and the results would be just as effective. This changed his classroom. The best readings for seventh and eighth graders have multiple subheadings and are limited to one page. This allows middle school students to process and collect information efficiently and effectively. Encourage students to find five or six important facts, one to two from each subheading. When the reading and discussion portions are finished, model the notes that you take as the teacher, so students can compare.

Adam

For middle school, students get more out of Cyber Sandwich when they read the same text and compare notes. This was extremely helpful for my seventh graders when they were studying the Magna Carta.

 Student 1

- King John was cruel and lost his temper easily. England went to war with france and lost. As a result King John lost a lot of land, he then placed heavy taxes on his nobles for losing the war.
- Nobles had had enough of the high taxes so they rebelled and overtook london. After they took over England King John negotiated with the nobles.
- King John met with the nobles in 1215 and signed the document called the Magna Carta. This granted them freedom and basic rights.
- Protection of church rights and other things were put in place
- Although King John didn't abide by the rules this set a foundation for the basic rules in england and the rest of the world for years to come.

 We both have!

King John signed an agreement.

England lost the war

Nobles had to pay very high taxes

 Student 2

England lost the war and had lost a lot of land.

1215 the nobles had enough of johns taxes and forced him to sign the document .

On june 15 they met at runnymede and signed.

He did not like signing the document but they forced him to do it.

Student 1 Notes READING LINK

- King John was cruel and lost his temper easily. England went to war with france and lost. As a result King John lost a lot of land, he then placed heavy taxes on his nobles for losing the war.
- Nobles had had enough of the high taxes so they rebelled and overtook london. After they took over England King John negotiated with the nobles.
- King John met with the nobles in 1215 and signed the document called the Magna Carta. This granted them freedom and basic rights.
- Protection of church rights and other things were put in place
- Although King John didn't abide by the rules this set a foundation for the basic rules in england and the rest of the world for years to come.

It's common practice to compare the Magna Carta with the Declaration of Independence or the Constitution, but students have very little background information on the latter two documents. Comparing either with the Magna Carta can be overwhelming. As a result, seventh-grade students can read the same document about the Magna Carta and discuss their findings. Focus on one topic at a time, one discussion, and build common vocabulary as they gain a solid understanding of the Magna Carta and its importance for the world.

Student 1 Writing

King John was cruel and lost his temper easily. England went to war with france and lost. As a result King John lost a lot of land, he then placed heavy taxes on his nobles for losing the war. Nobles had had enough of the high taxes so they rebelled and overtook london. After they took over England King John negotiated with the nobles. King John met with the nobles in 1215 and signed the document called the Magna Carta. This granted them freedom and basic rights. Protection of church rights and other things were put in place. Although King John didn't abide by the rules this set a foundation for the basic rules in england and the rest of the world for years to come.

Adapting for AP:

To earn the synthesis point on an APUSH Long Essay Question (LEQ), the writer must extend their argument by explaining the connections between a development in a different historical period, situation, or geographical area or integrate an approach (discipline) that is not the focus of the essay (such as political, economic, social, cultural, or intellectual history).

One student demonstrates this in a Bloody Sunday Russian Revolution Cyber Sandwich when they mention that the people of Haiti suffered under French rule like the Russian people suffered under Tsarist rule. This student is connecting different historical periods (1791 vs. 1905) and explaining worker exploitation as a common economic feature in both eras.

Modifications:

Changed Ideas

Instead of simply writing a paragraph, require students using your Cyber Sandwich to point out the details from the text that helped them form a new, deepened, or changed understanding.

Book Review

Give students three book reviews. One person reads each review and then tries to convince the others why their book would be the best one for high school students to read. These are great conversations to listen in on as students try to change each other's minds about whose book is better and for what reason. For an extension activity, ask the students to write a letter to the principal expressing their opinion on which book should be used in US history classes.

Scott

My students took these letters very seriously, and I forwarded a few of the best entries, so that the principal could personally respond to the students. This made them feel considerable ownership in their school.

The Frayer model is a handy tool for students to build a deeper understanding of many social studies topics and vocabulary terms and concepts. At the beginning of a unit, Adam and Scott love sharing a Frayer slide deck and building vocabulary knowledge through each lesson. However, this simple tool can be used for so much more than building student vocabulary.

According to John Hattie, vocabulary tools such as the Frayer model have an effect size of 0.67 on learning outcomes. That's 1.5 times the normal year's growth as compared to fill-in-the-blank worksheets. It's 17 out of the 150 learning strategies in his chart *Teaching Literacy in the Visible Learning Classroom*. All this with little teacher prep and divergent opportunities for student input.

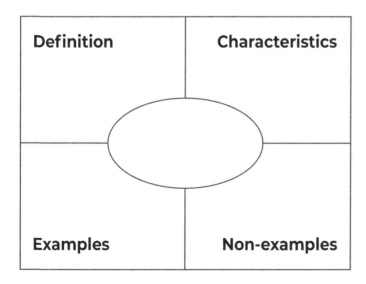

Description:

Dorothy Frayer and her colleagues developed the Frayer model in 1969 as a way to help students build vocabulary knowledge more efficiently and develop a framework for understanding the nuances of word meanings. With most vocabulary worksheets and comprehension-based questions, each student's thinking is narrowed down to one correct answer. The Frayer model's five-part graphic organizer format increases the possibility of correct and creative answers.

Marlena

What makes EduProtocols different from worksheets is the focus on divergent thinking (many possible answers) v. convergent thinking (one correct answer for all).

Using the Frayer model before a Cyber Sandwich is an effective teaching strategy to help students build background knowledge with vocabulary before engaging in the Cyber Sandwich. The more students interact with a text, the more information they will retain and recall for future use. Students skim the reading they will use for a Cyber Sandwich and make a word cloud list of unfamiliar words. (Use any readily available online program or a word cloud tool such as the one available at jasondavies.com/word cloud to create your word cloud.) Repeated words in a word cloud will be larger than others. As a class, choose three unfamiliar words and pair them with a Frayer. This strategy helps students build background information and prepares students for their reading during a Cyber Sandwich.

Academic Goals:

- Help students activate prior knowledge.
- Build connections with the essential characteristics of concepts.
- Develop an in-depth understanding of a word or concept.

Teacher Big Ideas:

- Simple for students or teachers to create and share.

- Great study tool for students.
- Helps organize large amounts of information.
- Creates a deeper understanding of content.
- Use whole-group or small-group discussion, or have students work independently as part of vocabulary development.

Prepare for the Activity:

Prepare for the Frayer model by creating a five-square template using paper or a slides program such as Google or PowerPoint, or have students create their own. The student or teacher labels the center box with the word or topic. The four outer boxes are labeled with a definition, characteristics, examples, and non-examples. To get started, you might choose the words that are used and type them in the middle of the Frayer. After enough reps, have students choose their own words.

Instructions:

Step 1: Prepare to distribute the Frayer in paper or digital format.

Step 2: Allow five minutes to Frayer a word.

Step 3: Students will complete the four outer boxes by adding a definition, three to four characteristics, three to four examples, and three to four non-examples. Images work well for examples and non-examples, as these visual representations will create powerful points of reference for students.

Step 4: Have students share their Frayer information with each other to deepen their understanding.

Marlena

The best non-examples are easily confused words or concepts. Encourage students to consider homonyms, multiple-meaning words, or similar but different concepts.

Key Points to Remember:

If you are making your own Frayer template, add bullet points to each box to prompt students to provide more than one answer.

Pressed for time or need to stop the cut-and-paste cycle? Frayer models are super easy for students to make on paper.

ELL Tips:

The Frayer model is a powerful tool to help ELLs organize vocabulary, historical people, or concepts presented in class. Not only does the Frayer model help students learn the definitions of unfamiliar words, it activates their prior knowledge on the concept, links it to new ideas, and helps students think deeply about applying their new words in new contexts. Further, asking students to explain the visual images and icons they put onto their Frayer model actually helps cement the word into their long-term memory. Explaining these choices helps them move beyond Basic Interpersonal Communications Skills (BICS) to Cognitive Academic Language Proficiency (CALPS).

Adapting for AP:

Don't overlook the power of the Iron Chef jigsaw when asking students to Frayer historical figures who frequently appear on assessments. For instance, a 2019 released DBQ asked students to evaluate the extent to which the Progressive movement fostered political change in the United States from 1890 to 1920. Asking students to Frayer the Progressive accomplishments of Jane Addams, Teddy Roosevelt, Julian W. Mack, Hiram Johnson, and others would give students valuable practice in making historically defensible claims and describing historical context relevant to the Progressive movement. While this may be difficult at first, students will improve with practice and even be able to transfer this skill to other areas, like analyzing Supreme Court cases or evaluating important pieces of legislation.

Modifications:

Iron Chef the Frayer

Use the Iron Chef format for the Frayer by assigning a team of four students a group of words. Each student in the team creates a Frayer for one or two of the words. The work is quick here, as each student is only creating one Frayer, but together the team is responsible for knowing all of the words. Allow a few minutes for team members to explain their word to the rest of the team before moving on to the next segment of the lesson.

SEE-IT Model

Instead of using the traditional Frayer categories of define, characteristics, examples, and non-examples, mix up the categories with a SEE-IT model, which was adapted by educator Julie Stern (@JulieHStern). SEE-IT is an acronym: State, Elaborate, Exemplify, Illustrate, and Talk. With many concepts and vocabulary words to cover in social studies, students must do more than simply write a definition. This strategy fits perfectly with a Frayer model and has students explain and expand on the meaning of social studies vocabulary and concepts as they learn new words.

Scott

Changing two of the Frayer descriptors from people with similar and different characteristics to successes and failures can help students deepen their historical research skills.

Adam

With the SEE-IT model, have students create 3–4 examples, then share them with each other.

State (Define)

The stamp act of 1765 was an act of the parliament of Great Britain which imposed a direct tax on the British colonies in America and required that many printed materials in the colonies.

Elaborate

Specifically, the act required that starting in the fall of 1765, legal documents and printed materials must bear a tax stamp provided by a commissioned distributors who would collect the tax in exchange for the stamp

WORD:

Stamp Act

Facts/Characteristics

- The taxes for the Stamp Act had to be paid in British money
- They would not take colonial paper money
- Massachusetts briefly experimented with the stamp duty before 1765

Illustrate

A modified student sample of a traditional Frayer

Adam

This is great to use when comparing historical people such as Thomas Jefferson and Alexander Hamilton or comparing presidents from different eras.

Scott

High school students can use the Frayer model to compare and contrast different economists or economic theories. It's sort of a way to use your superpowers to become a super nerd.

Frayer an Historical Person

Frayer an Historical Person was developed by social studies teacher Stacy Yung (@stacyyung). After sharing the template, students type the historical person's name in the middle box. Around the name, students add four icons or images to represent the person. Next, they add in four accomplishments. The last two boxes are saved for adding in other people who have similar and different qualities to this historical person.

A major part of the eighth-grade curriculum across the country is getting students to understand the Constitution and the founding principles of the United States. Themes include popular sovereignty, federalism, republicanism, individual rights, and checks and balances. Getting students to engage with this type of content is hard enough for even the most talented teacher, but getting students to understand and connect with government concepts is especially difficult. As social studies teachers, we need students to engage with informational texts and take away important information. The Sketch and Tell EduProtocol offers a creative, versatile, and visual solution for students to engage with social studies content. Visual thinking is deeper thinking.

Description:

To make a Sketch and Tell, students create an original drawing or diagram based on their response to social studies content like a video, an article, or the textbook. Some students may require specific prompts like "How does a bill become a law?" or "What is federalism?" Then students explain their original drawing to a partner, and finally, they write about their image or respond to a prompt about the concept.

Scott

Drawing and thinking lets students practice creating visual representations of historical events and the relationships that play out between historical figures and events. Hattie, Stern, Fisher, and Frey (2020) credit concept mapping with an effect size of 0.64 for improving student learning. Being able to draw and explain the emotional impact or historical value of an image is a powerful skill for artists, poets, writers, and learners.

Jon

Sketch and Tell is not a drawing lesson—art skill does not matter. Don't emphasize shading, perspective, or proportion. Sketch and Tell is about modeling a schematic of the essence of the lesson, which is also a STEM/STEAM concept, with students using visuals to explain the learning, while also explaining by writing.

Check out Adam's federalism lesson.

Academic Goals:

- Build students' understanding of an informational text by having them create images.
- Develop explanatory writing with informational texts and videos.
- Support students' understanding of informational texts by having them read with a purpose.

Teacher Big Ideas:

- If an image is worth a thousand words, creating the image is worth ten times as much! Force students to think through each part of the image they are creating by using the drawing tools in Slides.
- Draw and tell before writing allows processing time for students.
- A collection of images by a group or the class allows students to compare (and improve upon) their perception.

Prepare for the Activity:

Step 1: Prepare a Sketch and Tell slide deck with half the slide for the drawing and half the slide for the writing.

Step 2: Share the slide deck with students.

Instructions:

Step 1: Briefly review a linked informational text (online or textbook), slideshow, or video.

Step 2: Review the prompt or question to which the students will be responding.

Step 3: Allow five to ten minutes for reading text or two minutes for viewing a video clip, then give students ten minutes for creating, five minutes for a pair-share, and then five minutes for writing and telling.

Tip: Make sure students know how to use the drawing tools in their platform, as using Google or premade images in a Sketch and Tell is strongly discouraged. The point is to slow down students' thinking by forcing them to recreate the image in their mind one part at a time.

ELL Tips:

The Sketch and Tell EduProtocol was originally designed by Marlena to prepare students for the California English Language Development Test (CELDT), which tests students on their English proficiency in California. Students are asked to listen to an audio story, oftentimes a detailed explanation of a process above their grade level, and then retell the steps in their own words. Marlena was exposed to the released test questions in her training for work, and she immediately recognized the struggles students would have with this portion of the test. Sketch and Tell was developed to allow students the opportunity to sketch the "story" before explaining it to a partner. This drawing step allows students to process information and attach words they know to the retelling. It also allows them a space to define new words before retelling.

Scott recalls the first time he administered the CELDT test in California. There is a portion of the test where the administrator holds up a picture and the student must provide the name of the object in English. In this case, the image was of a microscope. He knew what it was, and the student knew what it was, but the student couldn't come up with the word in English, so he just smiled at Scott. That taught Scott the power of learning via Sketch and Tell. Visuals have more appeal than plain text to ELL students. Research shows that these learners respond to visual information faster when compared to text-only materials. Images are stored as a long-term memory, which helps students with vocabulary retention and recall. Ever since then, Scott has been using Sketch and Tell as a way to reinforce this visual vocabulary-language connection and acquisition.

So how can you leverage the Sketch and Tell to benefit English language learners? Front-load student vocabulary with Fast and Curious or a Frayer, and then use Sketch and Tell often!

Adapting for AP:

This concept seems elementary, but when you add in some content from AP Econ like market corrections, the invisible hand, or the Laffer Curve, you can dramatically up the challenge for your students. We'll discuss stacking later, but doing this with Sketch and Tells to help students learn the social studies vocabulary they will need to succeed on the AP test can be easy, creative, and fun. Don't ditch the collaborative aspect that makes Sketch and Tell so powerful.

Classroom Example:

Adam and Scott love using Sketch and Tell at the beginning of a lesson with major concepts in social studies. For example, understanding the major concept of feudalism during a Middle Ages unit is extremely important in seventh grade. At the beginning of

the Middle Ages lesson on feudalism, share a Sketch and Tell slide deck with your class. On the directions slide, provide two links and give students the choice to watch a video on feudalism or complete a one-page reading. Then offer a creative constraint like "Sketch what you learned about feudalism without recreating the social hierarchy pyramid."

Modifications:

Low-Tech

Sketch and Tell can also be a low-tech version of Pear Deck's Flashcard Factory. Assign students vocabulary words or social studies content, and give them a small amount of time to complete visual depictions of the definitions. Think about having a Fast and Curious Quizizz ready so that students can see how well they improve their scores before and after the Sketch and Tell activity.

AutoDraw

The Sketch and Tell EduProtocol can be used to help students formulate responses to texts, art, and movies. Use AutoDraw (AutoDraw.com) to provide an alternate format for students. Encourage students to create elements that they then copy onto their Sketch and Tell slide to create rather complex drawings.

Mold and Tell (Play-Doh) Version

A major concept for seventh-grade social studies is the political and social system of feudalism used during the Middle Ages. Students easily understand the social hierarchy pyramid. However, in this lesson, challenge the students to create their own representation of feudalism without making the pyramid. Give them Play-Doh, provide a creative constraint, and watch them think.

Adam

Sketch and Tell allows students to creatively show their understanding of abstract social studies concepts such as the invisible hand or popular sovereignty and explain these ideas in more concrete ways.

Marlena

Providing the option of a reading selection or a video of the same content is in alignment with Universal Design for Learning (UDL) where we provide more than one input method and make that option available to all students.

Adam

When using Play-Doh or Legos, it's important to give the students a 15–20-minute time limit to be finished in class. You don't want Play-Doh sitting out all night or Legos filling up space in your room.

Sketch   Tell

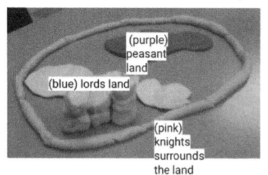

In europe the knights would surround the land to protect everyone and keep them safe. The purple represents the peasant land, the peasants were gifted the land by the lord. The lord's land is the blue, which are the nobles and the king. They gave knights and peasants land.

Build and Tell (Lego) Version

In this example for Sketch and Tell, Legos provide the medium for student understanding. When learning about the first Industrial Revolution in the United States, students began the lesson with a gallery walk reading, note-taking, and learning about different inventions. Students then create a Sketch and Tell about an invention they felt had the largest impact on the United States.

I made a steamboat. A steamboat is a boat that sails upstream to carry goods. It was invented by a man named Robert Fulton. This invention was so life changing because it moved goods into factories quicker, making them widely available for the consumer. Foods, and other necessities would not get places if it weren't for the steamboat.

Pair Cyber Sandwich with Sketch and Tell

In this lesson example, students learned about Muslim innovations during the golden age of Islam. Providing choices for lessons involving inventions and innovations from ancient civilizations sparks engagement for students. Students chose a Muslim innovation, collected five important facts, and discussed it through a Cyber Sandwich. Instead of a summary, students created a Sketch and Tell to show what they learned.

Stacked Sketch and Tell

Marlena uses Sketch and Tell as a collaborative activity for students. As a group, students create one drawing. Then students paste the drawing on each slide of the group where each person writes their own explanation. So all the students have the same image, but each has their own explanation or telling that they need to do with the group image. This modification encourages group discussion and consensus and is helpful for project planning and ensuring comprehension.

Chapter 11
Iron Chef EduProtocol

"History," said Mark Twain, "is just one damned thing after another."** Most students get that same sinking feeling when looking at the list of people, places, and events they need to memorize in a standard textbook. Iron Chef is a simple but powerful way to jigsaw through a chapter or unit that won't make your students feel overwhelmed.

Iron Chef is your go-to EduProtocol at the beginning of the new unit. When appropriately scaffolded by the teacher, the students will divide the labor and create crowdsourced resources that help them learn to study and master massive amounts of material with consistent review and repetition. Adam and Scott have Iron Chef-ed Medal of Honor winners, battles of WWII, Cold War events, and even people their students will meet in the first hundred pages of the nonfiction book the class is reading. Mixing Iron Chef with Fast and Curious is a definite winner, especially when students are writing their own quiz questions. Iron Chef also serves as an anticipation guide before students read.

Description:

There are four parts to an Iron Chef slide:

1. A space for students to put their topic and their name
2. A large blank section for bullets of information or a paragraph
3. A spot for a photo
4. A secret ingredient, which can be a variety of creative endeavors, including a six-word summary, similar people or events, an MLA or APA citation of their source, a map, or a link to a timeline

You are limited only by your own imagination when you front-load your unit with the Iron Chef. With the easy prep of the Iron Chef lesson, students are able to engage in inquiry, flex their critical thinking skills, improve their reading comprehension, and sharpen their writing abilities. Put this into heavy rotation in your classroom.

Academic Goals:

- Replace lecture with student inquiry in a scaffolded process.
- Conduct guided or free inquiry on a social studies or historical topic.
- Identify relationships between people and concepts.
- Work individually or in teams.
- Report out findings.
- Synthesize or summarize large amounts of information

Teacher Big Ideas:

As the teacher, you will see student work unfold in the Iron Chef in real time. This allows you to immediately coach students up if they are going in the wrong direction. Scott remembers redirecting a student who was being asked to research conversative principles during a government lesson. Instead, he was writing about conservation principles on his slide. Scott had to explain that the words are similar but mean very different things depending on whether you are talking about politics or the environment.

Switch things up and have students present someone else's slide. This allows the writer to hear their words out loud. They will get a better understanding of whether their writing was clear or confusing.

Prepare for the Activity:

Step 1: Keep in mind that this is a jigsaw or collaborative small-group activity. Divide the content into equal parts, one

Marlena

Once students master the basic format, provide a blank slide with a list of "requirements" for that slide and let them create to their heart's content!

part per student in a group. Each group should have between three and six students depending on the natural breaks in the content.

Step 2: Establish the criteria for each slide. For example, title, reference, 5–8 bulleted points, one image, one quote.

Step 3: Divide the content into 4–6 separate but related parts. Prepare the slides with different content.

Step 4: Assign groups of students who will then follow the division of content you have outlined. For example, student one covers part 1 of the content, student 2 covers part 2 of the content, etc.

Tip for Organizing Students:

The Iron Chef is a versatile protocol that engages the whole class in summarizing social studies concepts and historical events. Scott typically exports his class roster to a spreadsheet and then simply cuts and pastes the list of terms, events, and historical figures he wants his students to research next to their names. This way, each student is already assigned a topic and a slide number, and there is no confusion or trespassing on someone else's slide. You can also ask students to add their first name and last initial to their slide to eliminate any poaching. Scott has had incidents of students "vandalizing" other students' slides, but once he shows them how he can see everything in the Google editing history, these problems quickly go away.

Jon

Iron Chef works great in Nearpod, too!

Instructions:

Step 1: Each team opens the slide deck that is shared among them.

Step 2: Each team decides who will complete which part of the jigsaw.

Step 3: Students take about ten minutes to build their slide. They must stop when the time is up.

Step 4: Students present their slides to the class in one- to two-minute presentations. The teacher, while making sure their "voice time" is less than then the students', oversees the presentations, being sure to clarify or direct attention to important facts or sections.

Key Points to Remember:

- This is your go-to protocol for covering masses of content quickly.
- This is not a research protocol; it is a summarizing tool. Provide the resources for students. Your textbook is a great start!
- Build in UDL (Universal Design for Learning) scaffolds with video resources to easily support your ELLs and struggling readers.

ELL Tips:

The Iron Chef protocol helps ELL students read the important parts of a text and prevents them from getting lost in the fog of minor characters and insignificant details. When ELLs realize they only need to know about a few of the historical figures in a chapter, the text becomes less intimidating. In short, the Iron Chef jigsaw simplifies the reading for your ELL students by chunking and focusing on the major players in a historical event. Frontloading a reading with an Iron Chef scaffolding activity will pay off in the long run.

Adapting for Middle School:

For middle school students, it is best to scaffold the Iron Chef as we did with the Cyber Sandwich. For each slide, it's best to have an informative, one-page reading. Students read and design a slide in ten to fifteen minutes or less. The Iron Chef can be scaffolded further by adding paired reading questions to the slide or having students include four to five important facts from the reading. As the year progresses, start to drop the scaffolds and have students

Marlena

The topic for each slide does not need to be written on the slides. It may be effectively outlined on the board with the criteria for each slide. Then just assign students a blank slide deck per group and let them get to work!

design from a blank slide, thus decreasing your prep time while increasing student creativity.

The jigsaw style of the Iron Chef works well with historical events or topics that can be divided into multiple parts. For example, during the golden age of Islam, it might not be engaging or productive to have students learn about *all* of the inventions of that era. Rather, have students choose a topic to focus on for their slide, and then have them share with the rest of the class. For the golden age of Islam, for example, ask students to choose an invention in science, geography, math, art, technology, or recreation. Once students design their slide, try having them record a presentation using Flipgrid, an effective tool for sharing as it allows students to record their screens and voices. Plus, it keeps all the recorded presentations in one location. Students then watch each other's presentations, take notes with a Frayer, and comment on their peers' work. Finish the lesson with a Fast and Curious. Instead of spending five days on the golden age of Islam, students will get more out of a targeted two-day lesson.

Adam

The Worst Presentation Ever EduProtocol (Book 1) is a great way to help students learn how to design slides for the Iron Chef.

Art

1. What contributions did muslims make to your chosen field?
2. Describe these contributions.

1. Muslims rejected the use of images of humans or animals in their visual art, especially religious art.
2. Geometric and floral design, calligraphy, and textiles
3. Art sometimes was religious, as in the beautiful illuminated manuscripts of the Qur'an.
4. Muslim weavers wove wool, linen, silk, and cotton into cloth, and then dyed it in bright colors.

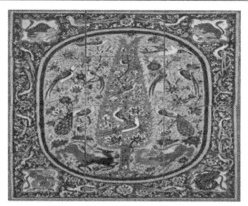

SECRET INGREDIENTS:

How are these contributions used today?

These art pieces are put in museums and people see in use these pieces all around the world.

#EduProtocols   #IronChef

Modifications:

Double Iron Chef

A Double Iron Chef is a jigsaw that covers two topics in one class at the same time. Assign half the class one topic broken into four parts, and the other half another topic broken into four parts. This will allow a faster-paced classroom for middle school, high school, and AP students. Be sure to share all of the slide decks back with all of the students so that each student can be responsible for all of the content. Also encourage note-taking during the presentations, just as students would do if the teacher were lecturing.

Solo Iron Chef

When Adam was looking for ideas to use with the Articles of Confederation, Jon suggested a Solo Iron Chef. Pure genius! Break up sections of a textbook or article into three to four sections, add in some guiding questions, and have students create their own personal Iron Chef in one class period. This is great for a standalone lesson like the Articles of Confederation, or it can be used as an end of unit review or assessment.

Visit Adam's blog to learn more about the worst presentations EVER!

Articles Of Confederation

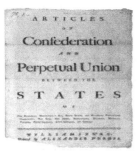

Secret Ingredients:

Why do you think America's first government was created to be weak?

They did not want the people to think of them as a tyrant or an oppressive government. As they just fought a long war to gain freedom from a oppressive rule.

Articles of Confederation - List 4 Weaknesses:

- Congress had a hard time passing laws as 9 of the 13 states had to agree on it.
- There was lack of national court system so states had to handle their disputes between themselves.
- There was no single currency used between the nation.
- Congress did not have the power to collect taxes so paying of war debt was very difficult.

#EduProtocols eduprotocols.com

Study Guide

For a pre-reading activity, we used the historical figures in *The Professor and the Madman*. Students researched the individual, noted key details and page number(s), and for the secret ingredient added what their classmates should know or remember about the person. As a result of the activity, students will take away their own study guide that they can refer back to and add to as they read.

THOMAS BLOUNT
Sheliya T.

"Or else the creators of these hard-word books put forward explanations that were complex...as in a book called *Glossographia* by Thomas Blount..." (pg. 86)
-Contributes to the story because he also published a dictionary (not as good as the OED)

- Lexicographer
- His principal works include *Glossographia: or, a dictionary interpreting the hard words of whatsoever language, now used in our refined English tongue* (1656)
- Aimed to define and explain unusual terms that might be encountered in literature or the professions
- The first dictionary to include illustrations and the first to cite sources for definitions
- *Glossographia* declined in fame when *The New World of Words* by Edward Phillips was published in 1658

SECRET INGREDIENT: WHAT SHOULD WE KNOW ABOUT THIS PERSON?

- Was a devoted Roman Catholic, which interfered with his profession when Catholics were excluded from the public areas of London

#EduProtocols   #IronChef

First-Person Narrative

The next step in this modified version is to have students turn their slide research into a first-person narrative. Even if students mostly copied information from Wikipedia into their Iron Chef slide, now they will embark on the literary heavy lifting of converting it from the third person into the first person. Finally, students create a quick screencast or Flipgrid of their work.

Scott uses this instructional sequence often. The repetition of reading about, writing about, and speaking about the same person three separate times helps make this knowledge sticky. Allowing

One of my principal works include *Glossographia: or, a dictionary interpreting the hard words of whatsoever language, now used in our refined English tongue*, that I published in 1656. Not to brag, but my dictionary was the first ever to include cited sources and illustrations. That's right. Get on my level. Oh wait, the Oxford English Dictionary already did. That's why they called me out in the book because I put forward explanations of complex words, but the OED went beyond and overachieved. How dare they compare me, I worked alone on that book while they were multiple contributors to theirs! Anyways, as a devoted Roman Catholic, my religion interfered with my work as a lexicographer because Catholics were excluded from some public areas of London. That sucks. You know what else sucks? That my dictionary declined in fame when *The New World of Words* by Edward Phillips was published in 1658! Who am I?

#EduProtocols   #IronChef

students a few days to watch each other's videos and then randomizing the videos and playing a "Who Am I?" game makes for fun formative assessment. These artifacts can also be big hits during Back to School or Parent Conference night. What parent doesn't like to see their child shine?

Recognizing the historical figures that students have presented about or heard about in class gives students extra confidence when they encounter them in the text. What would normally require hours of lecture, forced note-taking, and frequent quizzing can now be accomplished in three fifteen-minute sessions. We have used this technique to help students learn about historical eras, Enlightenment philosophes, and people in the civil rights movement. Adam reports that these activities have increased effort and engagement in his classes.

Adam

Ditching hours of lecture will buy you valuable time in class as the school year progresses. I earned three extra weeks of instructional time the first year I ran EduProtocols consistently.

Getting into the swing of things with Iron Chef took a few repetitions with our students. Now we think of them as lather-rinse-repeat. Share how you're using #IronChef in your class and with your subject matter with the #EduProtocols community on Twitter. In no time, you will find your own tribe of social studies teachers who appreciate your innovations.

Chapter 12
Number Mania EduProtocol

Description:

Number Mania is intended to replace a lecture-driven class segment with a quick, student-centered, efficient, and effective method of getting students rapidly up to speed with new content. The Number Mania infographic facilitates the creation of a visual representation of an historical event while synthesizing big-picture information quickly. Since students incorporate pictures and icons, infographics are easy to understand and an effective method for communicating statistics or significance related to an event or time period. Number Mania infographics can help students compare battles to decide which one had the most impact on a war, understand historical events such as 9/11, or develop background knowledge before a unit of study such as the overall impact of WWII. Number Mania can also be an excellent formative or summative assessment about an historical person, place, or event. Include this EduProtocol in stacking and sequencing routines because it helps students look at a reading or topic with fresh eyes and a strong sense of purpose. Pairing student-created visuals with content is a powerful way to help students retain facts.

Academic Goals:

- Determine the central ideas or information of a primary or secondary source.

Jon

A question I get a lot: What if kids submit the same fact? Easy! If I get December 7, 1941, nine times in a class of thirty kids, I will coach them to look more deeply. If I get the number of Japanese Midget subs several times, that's something that kids are interested in. We can make this into a Cyber Sandwich for tomorrow!

- Integrate and evaluate multiple sources of information presented in diverse formats and media (e.g., visually, quantitatively, and in words).
- Construct a visual and oral understanding of social studies content.
- Reflect and comment thoughtfully on the work of peers.
- Summarize findings.

Teacher Big Ideas:

- Infographics convey numbers and data in a visual format to increase comprehension.
- Students gain the big-picture idea of content before a unit of study.
- Students internalize the content as they analyze data and focus on the visual impact of the information.
- Data collection is crowdsourced, which speeds up the activity while still providing time for research.

Prepare for the Activity:

Step 1: Have students review a collection of infographics about history. (Try visual.ly/history-infographics or have them google "infographics history.")

Step 2: Ask students to explain which infographics contain valuable information and which ones are made up mostly of supporting details.

Step 3: Consider using a VEE diagram to help students with this. It is a great discussion starter.

Marlena

A Vee diagram is a visual representation of a complex phenomenon. In this case, the relationship to the important and less important factors in a historical event.

Important Details   Select at least 5   Supporting Details
                                     numbers on each
                                     side and explain
                                     your rationale.

Thesis/Summary Practice:
The most important details in this Number Mania are _____, _____, and _____,
because _____.

Step 4: Have students sort five historical infographics from most effective to least effective. The class should reach consensus on these five. Observe their process.

Step 5: Prepare the following:

- Curate a reading list or alternately allow students to conduct open web searches for information on the topic.

- Create a template with a collection of topic-appropriate icons for students to use. The Google add-on Icons for Slides or the Noun Project are good collections.

- Consider whether using a classroom shared spreadsheet is necessary for your class.

Tip: Use statistical websites like FiveThirtyEight, Pew Research Center, and USAFacts to help your students understand the depth and complexity of social science research. Include debriefing or peer review activities the next day so that students can self-assess their work or the work of their peers with a fresh eye. This also enhances

Ebbinghaus's spacing effect (spaced vs. mass learning), which enhances long-term memory when learning events are spaced apart in time rather than massed in immediate succession.

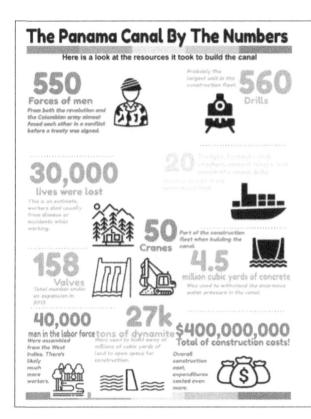

Through this assignment I've learned the actual purpose of infographics themselves. Which is that the data points usually all wrap up into one general point or storyline. The data points shouldn't be mindlessly or randomly put, because then where's the message? This was supposed to tell a story while mine just exclusively discussed resource numbers. My infographic doesn't really discuss a story, but through reviewing the debriefing document I have a better overall understanding of the general points of the history and building of the Panama Canal.

Instructions:

Make sure your students do 2–3 fun, nonacademic Number Mania activities before moving to academic content. These could be about favorite songs, movies, or the classic "What I Did Over My Summer Vacation." Thanks to Ryan O'Donnell (@creativeedtech) for his awesome "My Summer by the Numbers" template.

Step 1: Make sure to remind students that they are only to use the numbers from the reading you have provided (unless you are allowing for open research).

Step 2: Set a goal for the minimum number of statistics you would like to see presented on the Number Mania infographic.

Step 3: Students read and then collect facts on a shared spreadsheet. The class, in turn, draws upon this resource for facts when creating their infographic. This crowd-sourced step may be skipped if you are using the infographic development as a comprehension activity.

Step 4: Clearly decide and define your success criteria for Number Mania: a title, five or more facts with numbers, clearly organized information, creativity with colors and fonts, etc.

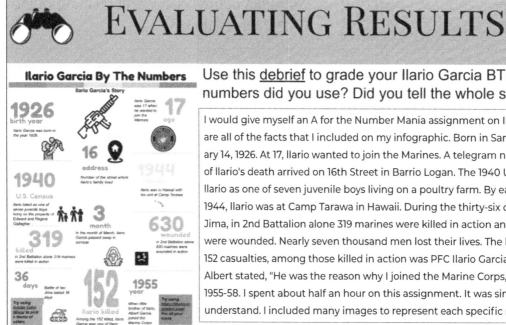

EVALUATING RESULTS

Use this debrief to grade your Ilario Garcia BTN. How many numbers did you use? Did you tell the whole story?

I would give myself an A for the Number Mania assignment on Ilario Garcia. Here are all of the facts that I included on my infographic. Born in San Diego on January 14, 1926. At 17, Ilario wanted to join the Marines. A telegram notifying the family of Ilario's death arrived on 16th Street in Barrio Logan. The 1940 U.S. Census lists Ilario as one of seven juvenile boys living on a poultry farm. By early November 1944, Ilario was at Camp Tarawa in Hawaii. During the thirty-six day battle of Iwo Jima, in 2nd Battalion alone 319 marines were killed in action and another 630 were wounded. Nearly seven thousand men lost their lives. The battalion reported 152 casualties, among those killed in action was PFC Ilario Garcia. Little brother Albert stated, "He was the reason why I joined the Marine Corps, serving from 1955-58. I spent about half an hour on this assignment. It was simple and easy to understand. I included many images to represent each specific number event.

Step 5: Give all students the same amount of time to complete the reading (ten minutes) contribute to the spreadsheet (five minutes), and assemble their infographic (fifteen minutes) if the icons are provided as drag and drop options. At the high school level, depending on the complexity of the reading passage, time needed may be longer. Adjust the time from thirty to forty-five minutes if needed.

Step 6: Ask students to verbally present one statistic from their infographic before they turn it in.

Step 7: Include a debriefing activity on the next instructional day. This helps students remember the content. Consider assigning a peer review activity for students who were absent and did not complete an infographic.

Key Points to Remember:

- Math involves sorting out ambiguities and providing clear definitions for comparisons. Our students need practice interpreting social science data sets. Number Mania provides a window into your students' critical thinking skills.

- Are students focusing on the first numbers they find in a reading, or are they looking for the big ideas that need further explanation? Or the numbers that will help to tell a specific story or substory? Students should follow a number-explanation-graphic format.

- Students should be able to explain why they chose these elements during the classroom debrief.

ELL Tips:

Visual illustrations and graphics help ELL students understand historical content while learning academic vocabulary germane to social studies instruction. Scott remembers a student who was struggling to complete an infographic on Adam Smith's invisible hand in capitalism. He didn't understand the word *wages* in the reading Scott had supplied. When Scott showed him the bag of money icon, everything clicked. As an extension activity, have your

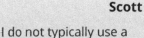

Scott

I do not typically use a Google Form or Sheet to crowdsource or focus on the statistics I want to see with my high school students. I want them to show me what they think are the important details. I include a debriefing document and self-reflection piece with Number Mania.

Adam

I use a Google Form in middle school because it helps students focus on submitting their own number to our facts sheet. After ten minutes, I will convert the Form data into a Google Sheet and share.

students write a short paragraph or summary of their topic, elaborating on the explanation blurbs they used to create their project.

Have students practice with sentence stems like "This is important because . . ." Supplying the beginning words for ELL students is an effective language scaffold.

Adapting for Middle School:

In middle school, we like students to use Number Mania as a way to comprehend historical topics on a deeper and different level. For example, when students are introduced to the Declaration of Independence unit, do a quick read where they focus on number-related facts. Students can then create infographics about the oldest and youngest signers, number of sections in the declaration, and important dates with the signing of the declaration. This big-picture approach is an easy way to front-load students on a topic before diving deeper later in the unit.

It's important with middle school students to establish clear learning goals and success criteria. Success criteria includes a title, five or more facts with numbers, clearly organized information, and creativity with colors and fonts, etc.

Marlena

Number Mania serves as an excellent entry into another activity based on research such as a formal report, persuasive essay, etc.

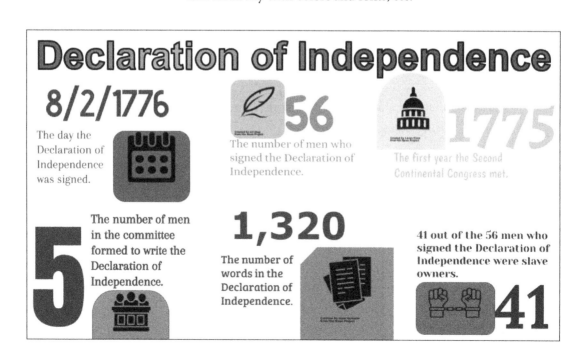

Number Mania also works well with students researching famous battles and wars. For example, students explored American Revolution battles and created Number Mania infographics with five important facts and icons. Students then explained why their chosen battle was important for American history. You can extend the Number Mania lesson and have students write a summary about their learning. You could also have them exchange their Number Mania infographics for peer review. Lastly, you could print the Number Manias and have students do a gallery walk.

Adapting for AP:

Number Mania assists students in developing the historical thinking skill of interpretation. This skill helps students describe, analyze, and evaluate the different ways historians interpret the past. When students analyze a historian's argument, they are able to explain how the argument is supported through the analysis of relevant historical evidence. When students create a Number Mania infographic, they are evaluating evidence and explaining relevance—key features that AP readers look for in historical writing.

Modifications:

After four to five reps with preselected icons for students, consider allowing students to find their own sources and format them in a bibliography or works cited page. This allows you to give students a minilesson on source authenticity and authority. Also choosing icons from the Noun Project, Flaticon, or the Icons for Slides add-on and placing them on the side of your template gives student work a standardized feel and allows the teacher to follow up on the big ideas that the students thought were the most important.

Scott

When students present their Number Mania, ask them why they chose to include a particular statistic and have the other students give their explanation of historical importance a thumbs-up or thumbs-down.

Check out Scott's class example for Ilario Garcia.

Adam

If your students are unfamiliar with Google Drawings, Google Slides, or PowerPoint, it is super important to get some reps in, along with some basic tips about the tool you are using.

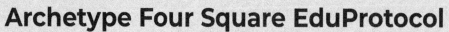

Chapter 13
Archetype Four Square EduProtocol

Description:

A few years ago, when Scott's students were learning about the excesses of King Louis XVI and the French Revolution, one shouted out, "Versailles sounds like Trump and his gold bathroom!" It was surprising to see a student equating excesses from one era to excesses of another. Scott did not know how valuable of an experience this would be until years later.

World history is full of archetypal characters and situations. Consider various revolutions: English, American, French, Haitian, Latin American, Mexican, Russian, African, not to mention more modern historical kerfuffles like the Cuban missile crisis, Watergate, and oh yeah, every presidential scandal. You don't have to have a doctorate in Jungian psychology to identify historical figures with personalities that have been prevalent since the dawn of time. If your students need help connecting people from the past to the people of today, this is the protocol for you!

The Archetype Four Square (AFS for short) protocol helps students apply what they have learned from a unit of study by sorting historical figures into conceptual tropes or familiar characters and situations. Characters might include the hero, the mother figure, the innocent, the mentor, the sidekick, the scapegoat, and the villain. Among the situations, we have the quest, the task, the hero's journey, the initiation, and the return.

Scott

This advanced critical thinking activity helps students practice transferring or applying knowledge from one subject to another. It is a useful lesson frame for eleventh-grade honors US history or APUSH classes that are taught to students who are also taking AP literature.

Academic Goals:

- Deepen analysis skills with historical figures
- Improve student elaboration on historical context and settings
- Strengthen social emotional learning by teaching social awareness, perspective-taking, empathy, appreciating diversity, and respect for others with social studies content

Teacher Big Ideas:

Collaborate with the other teachers at your school to expose students to as many examples of character archetypes as you can. Scott's science teacher can easily teach Madame Curie as a tragic hero or a groundbreaking feminist. His school neighbor is a Spanish teacher. When she reviews art and literature from the Mexican Revolution with her students, it is time for Scott to put on his helper cape and fly in to support her. In Scott's history class, students assess the importance of figures like Porfirio Díaz, Francisco Madero, Victoriano Huerta, Venustiano Carranza, Pancho Villa, and Emiliano Zapata. Students conduct inquiry around the time period of their leadership, their specific roles, political beliefs, allies and enemies, and ultimately their impact on the revolution.

For this assignment, he modifies some archetypal characters: the Strong Man, Robin Hood, the Elitist, the Rebel, the Romantic, the Wise Man, and the Traitor. You may find it helpful to design some graphic organizers to help students gain sufficient content knowledge to place historical figures into character and situational archetypes. You may wish to provide icons and definitions of terms for your students, so they don't spend too much time hunting for the perfect image.

Prepare for the Activity:

Make sure students have a wide variety of sources to consult when they review the accomplishments of their historical figures or situations. Students can practice identifying the steps in the hero's journey using a thirty-second political campaign video or radio spots. This does not have to be a text-based activity.

Provide students with a summary of the topic or content.

Mexican Revolution Archetypes

The People's Leader - Realized Constitutional reforms. Wanted Mexico to be completely socialist.

The Traitor - A person who betrays another or a cause. Orchestrated the ten tragic days.

The Strongman - Military dictator, ruled with an iron fist. Oppressed workers in name of profit.

The Theorist - Wealthy, educated. No leadership experience. Little crazy one.

The Rebel - Populist. Fights for the rights of the poor in Northern Mexico. Anti-US.

The Ancestral Spirit - Thought land gave life and people who work the land should own it.

The Muralist - Made public art that reflected Mexican identity and started a cultural renaissance.

The First Chief - A constitutionalist who rebelled against Huerta's government.

The Peacemaker - Only got involved in the Revolution after Madero's murder. Tried to unify Villa & Zapata.

The Nepotist - Used family connections to get ahead, participated in Decena Tragica.

The Muleteer - Transported goods all over Mexico, including weapons from the US. Loyal to Madero.

The Novelist - Wrote first-person accounts of the female experience in the Revolution.

The Musician - Short-lived president who helped overthrow Carranza and gave singing lessons during his exile.

The Puppet Master - Known for controlling things from behind the scenes. Also called El Jefe Maximo.

The Mover - Elected by Aguascalientes Convention. President for 2 months. Moved capital to San Luis Potosi.

The Lawyer - Marries wealthy Hacienda heiress. Partners with Madero. Named Secretary of State for Justice.

The Soldadera - A dedicated Villista, joined his army in her mid-20s. Hid female appearance. Vicious fighter.

Instructions:

Step 1: Provide students with a Frayer-like template a list of the characters or historical figures that they will need to sort conceptually into character or situational archetypes. Do not ask them to do both at the same time when you are starting out. That task is better performed with the Hero's Journey Protocol.

Step 2: Help students with their reasoning skills. This description makes it sound like Pancho Villa is a Robin Hood archetype because he wanted to take land from the Terrateniente and give it to the poor (peasants) or Villistas. Model as much as possible using figures from across the curriculum.

Step 3: Consider letting students work out their reasoning in small groups. They will argue over the definitions provided, and that is good practice.

Step 4: Remember, there are really no right or wrong answers here. This protocol hits all of the Four Cs but requires students to collaborate and communicate to apply their knowledge into a new conceptual area. Yes, some students may be off base. Try asking them some questions to steer them back on track instead of giving them the answers.

One image, icon, and emoji that represent this person (emojis, symbols, icons)	Archetype represented by this person
	The Muleteer - Transported goods all over Mexico, including weapons from the US. Loyal to Madero.

Pascual Orozco

Rationale/Support	Another representation
Orozco supported Madero in his presidency. Orozco worked as a muleteer for various mining companies. When Madero was looking for revolutionary leaders to overthrow Porfirio Diaz, Orozco joined him.	The Zion muleteers were a Jewish unit in the British army during the Dardanelles. They transported goods. The fighting force also carried food ammunition water and other supplies.

Key Points to Remember:

A mental model is a visual representation of how something works. Mental models help us understand complex thinking. They shape the connections we make with the world's intricacies. We use them to simplify complex ideas and ramifications. Hattie, Stern, Fisher, and Frey (2020) provided a mental model on learning transfer for social studies teachers. It uses a simple three-step process to help students grasp the structure of any subject or topic. First, students acquire understanding of individual concepts, then they connect two or more concepts in a relationship, then they transfer them to new situations. The Archetype Four Square asks students to use critical thinking, communication, collaboration, and creativity as they consider how their historical knowledge applies to new situations.

Adapting for AP:

Some students are so excited when they identify a connection between a historical figure and an archetype that they forget to explain why making the comparison is important. This is key when providing analysis. Tell your teacher what it means! Explain why this feature or aspect is so important. The end-of-year AP tests in history require students to identify, compare, and evaluate multiple perspectives on a given historical event in order to draw conclusions about the event. The AFS protocol allows students to practice this type of thinking in a low-stakes, collaborative classroom setting.

ELL Tips:

Despite deficits with academic vocabulary, second-language students are very familiar with the narrative structure. Narratives represent shared understandings of human experience. Narrative writing helps students develop audience awareness, organizational skills, and the ability to select and use specific, concrete details, all of which are key in informational and argumentative writing. In short, the AFS EduProtocol levels the equitable playing field in literacy instruction and helps students improve their writing with all text types.

The Archetype Four Square protocol will help students at all levels demonstrate that they can transfer their learning from one subject (English) to another (history). When students start to see that all of their subjects are connected, they become more engaged learners.

Adapting for Middle School:

Students in middle school will need quick, direct instruction on archetypes before this lesson is implemented. It's best to share a quick definition of the word *archetype* along with some student examples.

Students in a sixth-grade class used this lesson as a processing activity after a study of famous Egyptian pharaohs. The sixth graders did great with applying the archetypes to the pharaohs and using evidence and reasoning for their decisions. However, students struggled with connecting a modern-day person to the archetype. Practicing making connections across historical people and events is what the Archetype EduProtocol is all about.

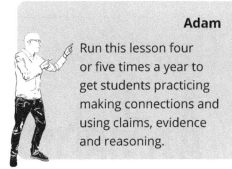

Adam

Run this lesson four or five times a year to get students practicing making connections and using claims, evidence and reasoning.

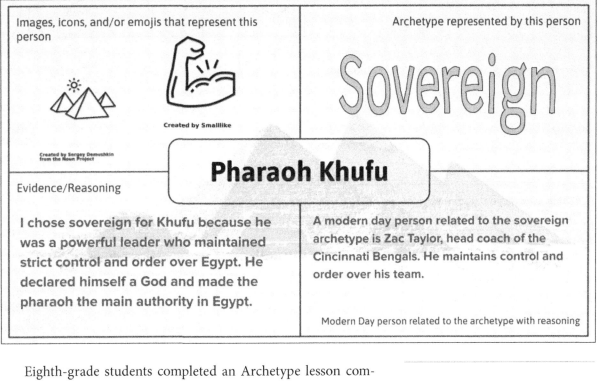

Images, icons, and/or emojis that represent this person

Created by Smalllike

Created by Sergey Demushkin from the Noun Project

Archetype represented by this person

Sovereign

Pharaoh Khufu

Evidence/Reasoning

I chose sovereign for Khufu because he was a powerful leader who maintained strict control and order over Egypt. He declared himself a God and made the pharaoh the main authority in Egypt.

A modern day person related to the sovereign archetype is Zac Taylor, head coach of the Cincinnati Bengals. He maintains control and order over his team.

Modern Day person related to the archetype with reasoning

Eighth-grade students completed an Archetype lesson combined with an Iron Chef. During this quick lesson, students could choose to read biographies about seven different founding fathers who were present at the signing of the Declaration of Independence. Students designed a slide based on what they learned about their figure. They listed five facts, included a picture, and applied an archetype character to their founding father. Since this was a quick lesson, the archetype characters were created to fit with the biographies of the signers.

The Supervisor - someone who is involved with a lot of committees and overseeing the development of our country.	
The Lawyer - someone who seeks justice and fairness in the law.	
The Jack of All Trades - a person who can do many different types of work	
The Radicalist - someone who is extreme in their views, and opinionated, loud.	
The Orator - a good speaker, good at getting others to listen and follow.	

Archetype - typical example of a certain person or thing.

After you research and read about these signers, discuss and decide which archetype would fit that person.

#EduProtocols eduprotocols.com

Which archetype represents your signer?

He was a Jack of all Trades.

Why did you choose this archetype?

Even though quiet he was very smart. He was fluent in five languages and was also a lawyer. He was also many more things such as agronomist, musician, scientist, philosopher, author, architect, inventor, and statesman. He was a very smart man and cold do many things.

Secret Ingredients:

Who is another person similar to your signer (modern day or historical)?

I think that he is like Lin Manuel Miranda. He can do many thing like write, play instruments, sing, act, and freestyle rap.

Created by Samuel Rosenzweig from the Noun Project

5 Facts about your signer:

- He was born April 13, 1743 in Shadwell virginia.
- He began the study of latin greek, and french at age 9.
- He attended William and Mary college.
- Even though he was quiet he was a valuable member to society.
- He was elected to the House of Burgesses in 1769. It was there that his involvement in revolutionary politics began.

#EduProtocols eduprotocols.com

Modifications:

Think of Archetype Four Square as a baby step toward using the Hero's Journey protocol. The teacher provides the narrative and asks the students to fill in the archetypal characters and explain why each historical figure represents that type. Teachers provide archetype definitions and icons, and students find pictures of the historical figures and add a three- to five-line explanation that describes how the character fits the archetype. Have students add a blank slide explaining their reasoning for each historical figure.

Adam

Don't get caught up in the "rules" of lessons. Think outside the box and create ways for the lesson to work with your students.

Chapter 14
Hero's Journey EduProtocol

The Hero's Journey as framed originally by Joseph Campbell in 1987 and clarified by Christopher Vogler in *The Writer's Journey* (1992) has long been a popular framework for narrative storytelling. Narrative writing often takes a back seat to argumentative and informational writing in history classes, and that is wrong on so many levels!

However, many social studies teachers are divided on the percentage of instructional time they should devote to the teaching of narrative, informational, and argumentative writing in the upper grades. The National Assessment Governing Board advises that narrative writing should decrease to about 20 percent by the twelfth grade. Other literacy experts, however, recommend that narrative writing should increase in all grade levels because of the benefits to English learners and improvements in student engagement at the secondary level.

The HJP is a concept sorting activity. A concept sort is a strategy that helps student label, classify, and organize the parts of historical events into a framework for better understanding.

The Hero's Journey EduProtocol (HJP) makes it easier for teachers to approach narrative writing in history. The HJP engages students in thinking about history as a narrative they can construct, which improves their buy-in and ownership of the curriculum.

The HJP is a complement to the Archetype Foursquare (AFS) in that while the AFS gives students practice in identifying character types and elaborating on their motivations, the HJP helps students identify situations involved in historic events and analyze the decision-making points within a narrative structure. These are essential skills in making historical connections and demonstrating chronological reasoning, both of which are assessed on year-end AP exams. For example, explorers like Ibn Battuta, Marco Polo, and Christopher Columbus all fit into Jungian archetypes as individuals, but collectively they have each walked every step of the Hero's Journey. Social studies students pursuing AP Capstone should be able to conduct multiple analyses of these individuals, shifting between discipline-specific terms from anthropology, archaeology, economics, geography, history, law, linguistics, political science, psychology, and sociology, demonstrating competency in multiple fields. Additionally, while some students may understand the Russian Revolution as a complex and multilayered historical event, other students may grasp it more easily as a Shakespearean tragedy with the Tsar's family in the role of Hamlet. Both of these protocols provide students with advanced critical thinking scaffolds for simplifying complex historic events.

Description:

The HJP is really a concept-sorting activity. A concept sort is a strategy that helps students label, classify, and organize the parts of an historical event into a framework for better understanding. Teachers provide students with a list of people, places, and events from the event. Then students place them into different categories and explain their decisions.

Academic Goals:

- Improve comparison skills between historical events.
- Boost narrative writing fluency in historical contexts.
- Elaborate on contextualization.

Teacher Big Ideas:

- Comprehensive timelines of an historical event lend themselves especially well to the successful completion of a Hero's Journey protocol.
- Use simplified readings instead of college-level texts. Instead of using excerpts from the Communist Manifesto or the Long Telegram, try SparkNotes.

Adam

The HJP provides the perfect opportunity for a transitional phrase mini lesson. Learning to add transitional phrases to the first draft will avoid leaps from topic to topic and strengthen student writing to help them assert their point of view more effectively.

Prepare for the Activity:

Step 1: Provide students with lists of participants in the historical event, as well as phases in the event that they might easily associate with steps in the Hero's Journey, i.e. preparing for the invasion, launching the invasion, advancing, retreating, etc.

Step 2: Using a shortened, six-step version of the Hero's Journey may be appropriate when scaffolding for elementary or middle school students, but don't be afraid to give high school students the longer twelve-step framework. It offers twice as many potential connections for your future storytellers.

Six-Point Model	Twelve-Point Model
Act I Call to Action Threshold	**Act I** Ordinary World Call to Adventure Refusal Meeting with the Mentor Crossing the Threshold
Act II Helper Abyss	**Act II** Tests, Allies, Enemies Approach to the Inmost Cave Ordeal Reward
Act III Transformation Return	**Act III** Road Back Resurrection Return with Elixir

Instructions:

Step 1: Show students a short YouTube video overview of the Hero's Journey, "What Makes a Hero?" by Matthew Winkler (You can find it here: youtube.com/watch?v=Hhk4N9A0oCA.) After watching, practice identifying the stages of the Hero's Journey using commercials or short nonverbal videos from the collection at the Literacy Shed (Literacyshed.com), or discuss how the Hero's Journey works in popular films from their childhood.

Step 2: Provide the template and readings to students.

Step 3: Ask students to map out the selected situations and "characters" on a blank storyboard.

Step 4: Provide ample discussion time so that students can present their explanations and rationale. Give enthusiastic and positive feedback. For example: "Characterizing Rasputin as a test is a very creative interpretation!"

Key Points to Remember:

Don't force the Hero's Journey into every historical situation. It is a framework to practice analyzing narrative, not a mandate to turn everything into a myth that can be assessed with a five-point rubric.

Don't be afraid to customize elements to make this easier for students. If there isn't a trickster or transformation in a particular historical event, don't include these terms in your materials.

Focus on the explanations, not the writing. The important part of the Hero's Journey EduProtocol is that students are taking risks by turning their historical knowledge into literary classifications. Reward risk-taking when you see it.

ELL Tips:

ELL students may find the six-step Hero's Journey map easier than the more challenging twelve-step journey outlined by Vogler. Remind students that the Hero's Journey is just a more elaborate framework for the three-act story structure (setup, confrontation, resolution). For example, for middle school, consider showing episodes of *The Simpsons* to review the beginning, middle, and end of stories.

Adapting for AP:

Many teachers use AP essential questions to help students prepare for the end-of-course exam. To what extent did the Watergate scandal create a constitutional crisis? To review for this question, ask students to complete a Hero's Journey story map of the Watergate scandal, emphasizing presidential actions that threatened the checks and balances between our branches of government. To complete this, students sort historical figures and events into the Call to Action, Threshold, Helper, Abyss, Transformation, and Return situational steps in the chart. There are not any right or wrong arguments; the goal is to have students practice explaining why they labeled a person as a certain archetype or identified them as enmeshed in a certain situation.

CITY OF THIEVES BY DAVID BENIOFF -- HERO'S JOURNEY STORY MAP		
Call to Action	Threshold	Helper
The Col. orders Lev & Kolya to find 12 eggs for a wedding cake (35).	The Kirov - Lev's childhood apt - is destroyed by German bombs (68).	Russian partisans save Lev from Einsatzkommandos (168).
Abyss	Transformation	Return
Abendroth punches Lev & draws his gun, fighting a bear (230-31).	Lev had shown a bit of courage, Vika kisses him and leaves (235).	Vika knocks on Lev's door (257).

Modifications:

As a Summative Assessment

Think of the Hero's Journey EduProtocol as a creative formative or summative assessment.

When used before a unit, the concept sort helps the teacher understand what students already know about the content. When used after a unit, teachers can assess their students' understanding of the concepts presented. Conceptual change programs that challenge students to elaborate on concept development by explaining examples and non-examples have a .99 effect size, according to Hattie. Thus, teachers who use the Hero's Journey EduProtocol consistently can expect to see more than two years of academic growth with their students!

Chapter 15
Retell in Rhyme EduProtocol

Responding to a text in writing has an effect size of .77 on reading comprehension. Writing personal reactions and interpreting texts can increase reading comprehension to support responding to text. In this protocol, students will use historical details from a text to create rhyming couplets. Students who like to rap or who enjoy writing poetry will excel with this protocol!

Description:

A few years back, Scott decided to try to make the death of Socrates more relevant to his ninth- and tenth-grade world history students by asking them to read an eyewitness account—what's known to historians as a primary source—and retell it in rhyme. They tweeted their rhymes. Afterward, students voted on the best examples by retweeting and liking couplets of their work.

The primary source used in our example, "The Suicide of Socrates, 399 BC," is located at eyewitnesstohistory.com/socrates. htm. Any rhyming dictionary, such as the one found at rhymezone.com, will support students as they write their couplets.

Students at the AP level should submit their version of the story in at least ten rhyming couplets. There may considerable variation in quality in the final products as some students will excel or be challenged differently in this activity. Regardless, the end results are sure to be highly entertaining!

Jon

Remember, an effect size of .40 is a normal year's worth of growth. So anything above .40 will positively impact student learning.

For the next step, provide students with twenty of the best rhymes and have them cut the list down to ten. Properly sequence them with a beginning, middle, and end. This scaffolding exercise will help students add concrete details to their formal essays.

RETELL IN RHYME
NAME OF POEM - HISTORICAL EVENT
BY STUDENT NAME

1	11
2	12
3	13
4	14
5	15
6	16
7	17
8	18
9	19

Student Example:

Death of Socrates

There stands Socrates in front of a jury
Five hundred Athenians worked up in a fury

Was the death of Socrates all his fault
Were the jurors of Athens bitter like salt

Socrates stood trial for corrupting the youth
He was found guilty of asking questions and revealing the truth

If he was found guilty
Death would be Socrates' penalty

Since he refused to recognize the gods of the state
The citizens treated Socrates with venom and hate

Socrates was seventy years old
The jurors indeed treated him cold
Socrates' death was not a suicide
The punishment was his to decide

His friends visited the jail and urged him to flee
But Socrates soberly told them that was not to be

While Apollodorus was weeping and drying his eyes
Socrates readily drank the hemlock and cheerfully dies

The account was written by Socrates' most famous student, Plato
He described the scene with the voice of a fictional character named Phaedo

Academic Goals:

- Help students determine the central ideas or information in a primary or secondary source.
- Build student confidence in playing with language, improve creativity, and inspire future poets and songwriters.
- Develop paraphrasing skills. ParaFLY may help students prepare for this protocol in the weeks leading up to its introduction.
- Students practice writing accurate summaries that describe relationships among key historical figures and events.

Teacher Big Ideas:

Many of our students want to be rappers and YouTubers. They seem to think that zero practice is required to master this craft. This protocol shows them that becoming the next Roddy Ricch or DaBaby will take daily practice, and the practice might even be fun!

Prepare for the Activity:

Find a reading that has a natural three-act structure, meaning a beginning, a middle, and an end. The textbook can be a good starting place. Scott also likes the firsthand accounts from eyewitnesstohistory.com because they have a wide selection going back to the ancient world.

Marlena

And some might even find they are good at it!

Instructions:

Step 1: Give students the same reading, and instruct them to construct an epic poem about the past. The poem should use only this source and contain at least ten rhyming couplets or twenty lines.

Step 2: Set a realistic timeline. Scott suggests thirty-minute blocks with student presentations of a few verses at the end of the period.

Step 3: Construct a chart for "grading" purposes and to give students an understanding of where their rhyming skills are compared to others in their class. Scott often allows students to self-report the number of couplets they have written on a Google Sheet roster of the class. This saves him a lot of time with data entry.

Scott

Sometimes I get out of control trying to measure student outcomes. A simpler metacognitive approach might be just to ask students which rhyme they think provides the most important historical details.

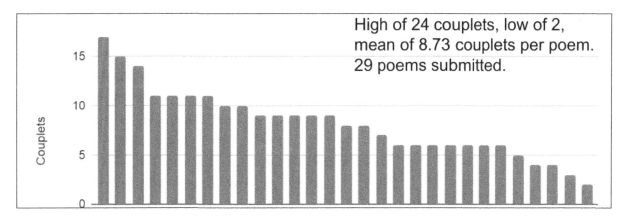

High of 24 couplets, low of 2, mean of 8.73 couplets per poem. 29 poems submitted.

Key Points to Remember:

This EduProtocol can be used as a formative assessment. The rhymes your students create will be the main or most important ideas they have pulled from the reading you provided. Do they tell the whole story of this historical event? Students who use insignificant supporting details may need some help in seeing the bigger picture.

Adam

Sometimes students get caught up with trying to rhyme a specific word and get stuck. Remind them to think outside the box and try other synonyms that are easier to rhyme. Or to move on and come back to that one later.

ELL Tips:

Robert Marzano (2004) has noted that the four disciplines that make up the social studies curriculum contain over 55 percent of a student's academic vocabulary. Using Rewordify.com can help students find synonyms for the difficult words they encounter in social studies instruction. Many students are shocked to discover that their favorite songwriters use rhyming dictionaries and cliché dictionaries to create their magical verses. Let them use the tools the pros use.

Adapting for Middle School:

Middle school students often cringe when they are asked to create a poem. Adam has observed that students often shut down after a few minutes of thinking. When he first asked students to Retell in Rhyme, he got the cringe look, but this time, they didn't shut down. Instead, the students started sharing rhyming ideas with one another. He finds Retell in Rhyme works best when middle school students can work in groups of two or three.

Before beginning a Retell in Rhyme, have students read a section from the text or informative primary source. In the following example, students read a two-page article on colonial regions. Students actively read and wrote down important facts and information in a graphic organizer. The information they collected was framed and focused with a question: "How did geography impact the way of life in colonial regions?" When the timer finished, students worked in groups of two or three to Retell in Rhyme the impact of geography on colonial regions.

Marlena

Allowing students to create with a partner will enhance their creative ability!

Adam

I like to use rhymezone.com when creating poems/rhymes because it's easy to use and well organized for middle school students.

RETELL IN RHYME
GEOGRAPHY IN THE COLONIES

1 Europeans were in Roanoke looking for freedom.

2 But Fernando got lost, and left 'em.

3 They were lost for awhile.

4 But they finally made themselves worthwhile.

5 They settled down in the East.

6 Until they worked up a feast.

7 So they set up some farms down in the south.

8 To feed some hungry peoples starving mouths.

9 Up in the north they created industries.

10 They made many different textile facilities.

11 Not to mention their beautiful harbors.

12 That promoted trade and order.

Adapting for AP:

Historical thinking involves the ability to describe, select, and evaluate relevant evidence about the past from diverse sources (including written documents, works of art, archaeological arti-facts, oral traditions, and other primary sources) and draw conclu-sions about their relevance to different historical issues. Retell in Rhyme helps students conduct an historical analysis of sources by determining which details are the most important and which are simply the easiest to rhyme.

Modifications:

Live Tweets

If some students need another option to Retell in Rhyme, or if your class is ready for a remix of the rhyming component, consider sug-gesting the class "live tweet" an historical news story.

Name: _____ Date: _____ Per:_____

Historical tweets are 140 character commentaries or summaries of an actual event. Many experienced Twitter users simply leave the vowels out of their words and write like they are sndng txt mssqs. For this activity, you must write 5 tweets. Be sure you skip spaces between words and use a space for punctuation. Tweets with less than 138 characters will not count. The hashtaas should inform you as to what the tweet will be about.

\#

\#

\#

Use the above worksheet for students to "live tweet" their retelling.

Scan the QR code for the Retell in Rhyme template.

Adam

For middle school students, I have found great engagement and success with the History Haiku.

History Haiku

A haiku contains three lines; the first and third are five syllables, and the second line is seven. A great way to start off the first five minutes of class is with the History Haiku. We learned this idea from social studies teacher Michael Matera (@mrmatera). As students walk into your classroom, before the bell rings, have a five-minute timer running with instructions on the board. Students follow the standard format for writing a haiku to explain what they learned the previous day. This is an awesome, creative way to get your students and class ready for learning.

Asking students to conduct original research often becomes a frustrating journey through Wikipedia. Students struggle to understand that one of the key values in academic research is the peer review. Scholars who clearly document their thought process and sources effectively shield themselves from accusations of plagiarism. Scott uses this protocol as a group collaborative activity with his classes first, before rolling it out as an individual assignment that students use to document their research process. Think of the Research EduProtocol as a collaborative Google Sheet or Microsoft Excel file on steroids. The information within the document is direct evidence of the efforts of your students. All of their efforts are tracked over time, enabling the teacher to see how hard they have worked at searching for and interpreting other scholars' academic work.

Description:

The Research EduProtocol was developed by Brigeen Houghton, a high school AP English teacher and master librarian. This protocol works well with all inquiry-based instruction, especially when it is used collaboratively to help students share and present their findings. While the original Research EduProtocol was geared toward helping students write research reports, the AP Capstone tasks vary from annotated bibliographies, team presentations, reflection portfolios, team projects, a presentation and an oral defense, to a 4,000–5,000-word academic paper featuring a student's original research and analysis. This is rigorous and time-consuming work that needs to be deliberately spaced and scaffolded to guarantee students will be successful in the Capstone courses and ultimately ready for the self-directed learning experiences they will have in college.

AP Seminar and AP Research are courses that Scott's school offers so that students may earn a special certificate or seal of distinction on their high school diploma. Students who earn scores of three or higher in AP Seminar and AP Research and on four additional AP Exams of their choosing receive the AP Capstone Diploma™. Students who earn scores of three or higher in AP Seminar and AP Research but not on four additional AP Exams receive the AP Seminar and Research Certificate™.

For this AP-level protocol, we will use the AP Capstone QUEST framework to teach students critical and creative thinking skills as they make connections between various issues and their own lives:

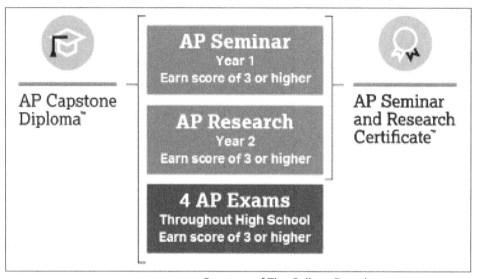

Courtesy of The College Board

Questioning begins with an initial exploration of complex topics or issues. Perspectives and questions emerge that spark one's curiosity, leading to an investigation that challenges and expands the boundaries of one's current knowledge.

Understanding various perspectives requires contextualizing arguments and evaluating authors' claims and lines of reasoning.

Evaluating an issue involves considering and evaluating multiple perspectives, both individually and in comparison to one another.

Synthesizing others' ideas with one's own may lead to new understandings and is the foundation of a well-reasoned argument that conveys one's perspective.

Teaming up allows one to combine their personal strengths and talents with those of others to reach a common goal. Transformation and growth occur upon thoughtful reflection. Transmitting requires the adaptation of one's message based on audience and context.

Academic Goals:

- Improve searching techniques, especially with academic databases vs. Google and Wikipedia.
- Learn how to frame a problem and situate it in a base of academic literature.
- Source textual evidence and explain how it supports an argument.
- Reduce plagiarism problems by teaching students to attribute their textual evidence with parenthetical (in-text) citations and APA/MLA works cited pages.

Teacher Big Ideas:

- Start with a collaborative challenge, then move to individual tasks. Students will invest more effort when they get to choose what they are researching.
- Scaffold for weaker students by allowing them to use crowdsourced textual evidence so they begin their writing tasks with the same research base as the other students.
- Flip this EduProtocol by giving students rich excerpts of textual evidence and then having them find it, cite it, and interpret it.

Prepare for the Activity:

Step 1: Develop an essential open-ended question, also known as a research question, that students will use to focus their

Marlena

Using shared research allows all students to begin the writing phase on a level playing field while ensuring the quality of student-gathered resources.

research. For this example, students find evidence to answer an essential question: How has wealth inequality changed throughout American history?

Step 2: Find a short video clip and/or a short reading selection to share to help clarify and provide a common background understanding of the essential question.

Step 3: Provide sources for students to read that help them choose one side or the other to select evidence on. These articles will give students some shared knowledge before they set out to find their own evidence.

Pro Tip: Websites like ProCon.org and AllSides.org offer valuable resources for this activity. Pew Research also does a good job examining multiple sides of an issue.

Step 4: Create a group spreadsheet for fact-finding. Students will place their findings in the spreadsheet using their number on your class roster.

The spreadsheet should include the following fields:

- Column 1: Name or ID number for students
- Column 2: Link to the source: Where can I find it?
- Column 3: Fact/evidence: What does it say?
- Column 4: Explanation: What does it mean?

The Research EduProtocol gives teachers a window into how students interpret textual evidence. Some students may require additional practice by sorting the evidence they've collected into categories for and against each side of the claim.

Instructions:

Step 1: Present students with the essential question to be researched.

Step 2: Watch the short video clip for background. Check to ensure everyone understands the essential question.

See examples of a Research EduProtocol about wealth tax.

Step 3: Provide students access to articles or media to analyze so that they can choose which side they will defend: for or against. Use close reading or annotation strategies that are already familiar to your students.

Step 4: Students will search for supporting information that helps them answer the essential or research question. They will add their findings to the shared spreadsheet. Citations should include the title of the article, title of the webpage/journal, URL, and date accessed. Typically, this phase takes between twenty to thirty minutes.

Step 5: As a class, in groups, or individually, depending on the age and ability of students, review articles for authenticity and their ability to respond to the research question. Students may "vote" on the best articles before moving on to the next step.

Step 6: Students write their summary, report, or essay using the best research from the shared spreadsheet.

Marlena

This is an essential step in training students to question suspicious sources of information.

Key Points to Remember:

- Discuss which search terms and databases were more successful than others.

- Review credible and noncredible resources before students begin writing. Which are from peer-reviewed academic journals, and which are from "Joe Bob's" website?

- Scaffold accordingly with your students. The first time you do this, consider a nonacademic topic like: What is healthier: cheeseburgers or burritos? After multiple reps, your students will be ready to tackle meatier issues.

Scott

My school asks each teacher to assign two annotated bibliographies per semester in each subject. This ensures that students at my school consistently know how to present their research to an audience.

ELL Tips:

Consider modifying with nontext sources for ELL students. Stories on *60 Minutes*, video debates, even podcasts like NPR's *Throughline* or *15 Minute History* can be helpful because they have transcripts and students can listen on a higher language level than they can read. This makes complex ideas more accessible and helps students navigate vocabulary and language patterns that are not part of their everyday speech (Fountas and Pinnell, 2012). Listening while reading helps ELL students have successful reading events, where they read with enjoyment and accuracy. Listening while reading has been shown to help with decoding, a fundamental part of reading.

Adapting for AP:

Using the Research EduProtocol with primary sources from different historical eras can help a teacher build great text sets for a Continuity and Change over Time (CCOT) essay. These essays are frequently found on the AP world history exam. Teachers can help students prepare for this by having them collect evidence on the same concept throughout different periods of time. Scott remembers a student who was able to make multiple connections about income inequality during the Civil War by using census data from the 1860s and 1900. This student meticulously documented how the median wealth of the richest 1 percent of southerners was more than three times higher than the richest 1 percent of northerners and that slave emancipation wiped out a vast amount of southern wealth. Forty years later, the richest 4,000 families in the United States had the same amount of wealth as the other 11.6 million families living in the US.

Modifications:

After collaborative practice with the Research EduProtocol, Scott developed a challenge for his students. Can you collect five different facts from five different academic sources in one class period? This activity lends itself to a concept sort where students rate the facts on a scale from interesting to boring.

Scott

The Research EduProtocol requires some creativity and scaffolding to implement successfully. Don't be afraid to take your students down the rabbit hole of research. Just remember that helping them craft an argument using the language of historical documents and published scholars is the end goal.

See an example of a Research EduProtocol.

SECTION 3

Making the Most of the EduProtocols

Chapter 17
Stacking

Protocol A + Protocol A + Protocol A

Description:

In *The EduProtocol Field Guide, Book 2*, Marlena and Jon discuss the value of stacking. This is a strategy beginners can use right away.

Stacking is the process of repeating one protocol to extend its ability to deliver content. For example, in Scott's AP Research course, students need to demonstrate their reasoning skills via four components: 1) situating, 2) choosing, 3) defending, and 4) connecting. They must be able to explain the context of their problem, explain their choices and what consequences they anticipate, then justify their choices to form a line of reasoning and describe intersections across disciplines. Scott has them do the Research EduProtocol four times to stack these elements together.

Research + Research + Research + Research

Adam's middle school classes use stacking for longer readings. One of the standards in Ohio suggests that students need to understand how the United States acquired territories such as the Louisiana Territory, the Oregon Territory, Texas, the Gadsden Purchase, and the Mexican Cession. Adam stacks five Cyber Sandwiches over three or four days to cover these individual topics. At the conclusion of the lesson, students have five summaries they can use to create an annotated map.

Jon

Repetitions and Four Cs are the magic of EduProtocols. This is where the Forgetting Curve comes into play. But we're not about drill and kill. EduProtocols embrace a Four Cs, divergent approach.

Check out student samples at eduprotocols.com

Protocol A + Protocol B
(For example: Iron Chef + Frayer)

Description:

EduProtocols are adaptable to any teacher, any classroom, and any student. They can be combined with other EduProtocols, they can be stretched, they can be shrunk. You are limited only by your own imagination when it comes to EduProtocols because they are made to be smashed together. There are no limits to your creativity. When Jon and Marlena created EduProtocols, they never envisioned how creative people would be with them.

Smashing EduProtocols refers to blending two EduProtocols into something slightly different, to be used as one activity. Think of a Frayer used in the Iron Chef jigsaw style. Four students working together to complete a list of vocabulary words or concepts. Or perhaps a Cyber Sandwich ends with a Sketch and Tell for the reflection instead of a written summary. Smashing is using two EduProtocols, together, in a new way.

Robert Mayfield (@MrMayfieldRHS) needed a quick, highly collaborative vocabulary exercise for his geography classes, so he took two classics, Thin Slides and Iron Chef, and smashed them together. The Thin Chef was born. Infused with the Four Cs, students work in small groups completing one slide each by incorporating two words and pictures addressing a prompt supplied by the teacher. Students build their slides in seven minutes followed by

Marlena

Don't get intimidated by the names Smashing and Rack and Stacking, just know you can use the protocols in combinations to enhance your learning objectives and keep students highly engaged with new twists.

quick, two-minute group presentations. Robert found it especially helpful to use Thin Chef early in the week to supplement the vocabulary practice students had received following multiple rounds of Fast and Curious.

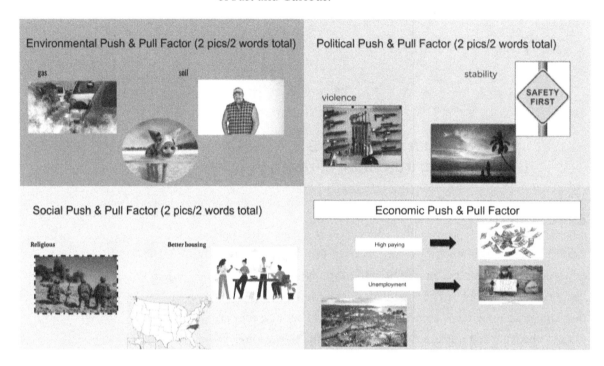

Teacher Big Ideas:

When creating with EduProtocols, it is helpful to remember the acronyms PROTOCOL and SPIRIT to guide you in your experimentation.

PROTOCOL reminds us of the essence of what makes a EduProtocol an EduProtocol. These are the key points that make EduProtocols work in the classroom with real students!

Protocol: a lesson or sequence of protocols equivalent to a lesson

Replicable: the structure can be repeated by students and other teachers

One to one: accountability for every partner when collaborating

Time: lesson frames can be used within a class period

Overtly connected standards: one protocol contains lots of standards

Marlena

There are actually some rules, but once you know the rules well and can apply the rules with fidelity in your classroom, you can break them!

C's in action: collaboration, critical thinking, communication, creativity

Open: can be used across subject areas

Loved: designed to be irresistible for students

SPIRIT:

SPIRIT captures our resolve for success when we use EduProtocols. Deploy EduProtocols with your students using these fundamental tools to build toward a positive outcome for your students.

Serious commitment: benefits happen over time, so stick with it

Progression: start slow to go fast; first attempts should be low-cognitive-load content

Immediate feedback: EduProtocols are more effective with quick feedback, often in real time.

Reps: Move away from an ineffective one-off activities to learning through repetition

Interest: keep it fun and engaging

Tech balance: pace your class through the use of technology

Smashing Examples:

One of our favorite smashes is the blended Iron Chef and Frayer. This is easy to set up. Simply add a bunch of Frayer templates to one slide deck, assign the vocabulary words, and assign four students. Let them divide up the words and Frayer them as a team. Each student is still responsible for all of the words, but the heavy lift of finding information and creating the slides is shared among the team.

Middle school teacher MaryKay Thede created an awesome EduProtocol smash with a Cyber Sandwich during a geography lesson about Athens and Sparta. She had students read and take notes about the impact of geography on Athens, Greece. The students collected and compared notes. Instead of a summary, she

Scott

Smashing might mean using Cyber Sandwich to practice collecting and analyzing textual evidence instead of summarizing as it was originally intended. Or adapting the Cyber Sandwich into an argumentation tool (pro and con) instead of a reading and summarizing comprehension check.

Adam

When you introduce a new EduProtocol smash, make sure you are crystal clear with your directions, otherwise students may revert to doing what they have always done with the protocol.

Marlena

Stacking is one of the true magical qualities of Eduprotocols. Same activity, change the content. This means low cognitive load for kids, quicker completion times, and LESS PREP for teachers.

Jon

According to the Forgetting Curve and Dr. Pfiefer's research, nothing cements content like more frequency of practice. Duration is not as efficient.

Scott

Oftentimes teachers get caught up in trying new ideas exactly as prescribed by a book. I have learned to adapt these ideas to the needs of my students. Sometimes you have to destroy the box in order to think outside of it.

Scott

When I get to the end of my school year and I am still in the Vietnam War, I panic and think I'm the worst teacher in the world. EduProtocol smashing helps me leap over tall content standards in a single bound. I literally cover both the Gulf War and the Afghanistan War in one day.

had the students draw an impact of geography through a Sketch and Tell. Students completed the Cyber Sandwich remix with an explanation of their creation through Flipgrid. By adding the Sketch and Tell to the end of the Cyber Sandwich, students used their notes to create a visual representation of geography followed by a verbal explanation.

ELL Tips:

Smashing EduProtocols gives you license to eliminate the difficult parts your students struggle with. A sheltered ESL teacher loves using Cyber Sandwich, but they think the most important part is the discussion between the two students. These students loosely use the Venn diagram for their discussion and leave off the summary paragraph because their teacher wants to hear them practicing academic vocabulary in conversational English. A Flipgrid response adds another speaking layer for ELL students that does not require writing. Purists may point out that this tip runs counter to the purpose of the Cyber Sandwich, which prioritizes discussion before writing for ELLs, but remember, you are the leader of your classroom. Feel free to smash and adapt these protocols to your classroom objectives.

Adapting for AP:

You may find these free high-quality resources helpful for your class. Many college instructors are sympathetic to the high cost of corporately published textbooks. Often, they turn to Open Education Resources (OER). The OER Commons (oercommons.org) uses an OpenStax hub (openstax.org/subjects/social-sciences) to offer peer-reviewed social science textbooks for free.

The Big History Project (bighistoryproject.com) uses a multidisciplinary approach to teaching fourteen billion years of history to middle and high school students. They also offer a standards-based world history course (oerproject.com) that builds historical thinking skills in preparation for the rigor and complexity of AP coursework. Take a look at these free resources and think about how this high-quality content can be easily smashed with your social studies EduProtocols.

Chapter 19
Racking and Stacking

A sequence works in a way a collection never can.

—George Murray, Canadian poet

Protocol A + Protocol B + Protocol C

Racking and stacking refers to pairing or combining two or three different EduProtocols over one or more class periods. This often helps students build background knowledge through different levels of learning and leads to a culminating project or assessment. We both began smashing EduProtocols with a classic—a Fast and Curious and Cyber Sandwich combination. It was after we added a Frayer and/or Sketch and Tell to the mix that we began a deeper dive into the content.

When you begin racking and stacking combinations of EduProtocols, ask yourself, "What do I want the students to be able to know and do?" Racking and stacking can be created to emphasize and sharpen specific critical thinking skills. One such EduProtocol stacking sequence helped Scott's tenth-grade world history students research and write about women who served in World War II.

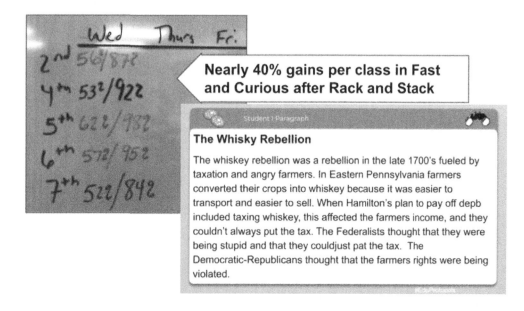

Nearly 40% gains per class in Fast and Curious after Rack and Stack

Student 1 Paragraph

The Whisky Rebellion

The whiskey rebellion was a rebellion in the late 1700's fueled by taxation and angry farmers. In Eastern Pennsylvania farmers converted their crops into whiskey because it was easier to transport and easier to sell. When Hamilton's plan to pay off depb included taxing whiskey, this affected the farmers income, and they couldn't always put the tax. The Federalists thought that they were being stupid and that they couldjust pat the tax. The Democratic-Republicans thought that the farmers rights were being violated.

Marlena

Shorter Rack and Stacks can happen within one class period as well. I love hearing about how Adam completes a Fast and Curious, Cyber Sandwich, Sketch and Tell, and another Fast and Curious all within one class period! Read on to see Adam's example.

Iron Chef + Sketch and Tell + ParaFLY + Frayer an Historical Figure

Racking and Stacking with Scott:

Before starting this project, Scott asked his students to tell him what they already knew about the 350,000 American women who served in World War II. After some awkward silence, his students couldn't name any of them. Not one! Rosie the Riveter did come up, but he dismissed her because, technically, she's just a recruitment poster.

Day One: Iron Chef

This was a perfect starting point for an Iron Chef inquiry lesson. It required collaboration, because once a student called out a female service member, no one else could research her. Students were asked to write a paragraph about their research subject, provide a photo, and for the secret ingredient reveal their source. This was so Scott could see how many students had advanced beyond Wikipedia to use the academic databases his school's digital library provided. Hint: not many.

Virginia Hall
Brielle F.

Virginia Hall was an American spy who assisted in the winning of WWII. She worked for the British at first, and then moved on to work for the Americans. She worked a clerical job at the U.S. consulate in Turkey. She also suffered a hunting accident where she shot herself in the foot. Gangrene infected her and she eventually had to amputate her left leg. After amputation, she learned how to use a wooden leg. This event got her the nickname "Limping Lady". She was the first British spy sent into Nazi-occupied France in 1941.

SECRET INGREDIENTS:

'A Woman Of No Importance' Finally Gets Her Due

Day Two: Sketch and Tell

The next day, Scott asked students to think about the most interesting fact they learned in their research and to turn it into a creative title for a book. This task was a natural fit for Sketch and Tell. Although he usually doesn't let them use Google images because he prefers that they draw original art, he made an exception this time so they could conceptualize something big about their WWII heroine. After their work time was up, each student pitched their book to the class. Some of the standout titles were: *An Angel in Hell, Female Super Spy, Hitler's Favorite Pilot, The Lady Named Death, The Princess Spy,* and *Tortured by the Nazis.* This got students excited about the next step.

Day Three: ParaFLY

On day three, Scott threw a curveball at the students and told them that the book they were writing was actually a children's book and it would have to be written at or below the sixth-grade reading level. Scott gave them some direct instruction and demonstrated the Hemingway App and Rewordify. Then he asked them to demonstrate their paraphrasing skills with 150-word excerpts from their sources.

Images that represent this person
(emojis, symbols, icons)

Virginia Hall
Brielle F.

Accomplishments

- Made an honorary MBE (Member of the Order of the British Empire)
- received Distinguished Service Cross, only award given to a woman in World War II, from American government
- French awarded her a Croix de Guerre to honor her work in occupied France
- placed into the Maryland Women's Hall of Fame in 2019
- Remains one of the most honored and most effective spies in American History

People that have similar characteristics or qualities

- Marie-Madeleine Fourcade
  - Worked for the French, leader of the largest French Resistance network "Alliance"
- Jeannie Rousseau
  - spoke five languages and at age 20 began working as a German translator

People that have different characteristics or qualities

- Klaus Barbie
  - infamous Gestapo (official secret police of Nazi Germany) chief who tried capturing Virginia Hall
- Any Nazis
  - Hall was a well wanted "fugitive", especially to the Nazis

---

Day Four: Frayer an Historical Figure

On the final day of in-class time, students were asked to complete a Frayer EduProtocol. This required them to conceptualize their research subject with icons, list their accomplishments, and identify people who are both like and unlike them. This proved difficult for some students, who lacked enough background information to identify people who were similar and different to their historical figures.

Day Five: Final Product from Book Creator

At the end of this project, Scott's tenth-grade world history classes had created forty-five children's books about individual women who served in World War II using Book Creator (bookcreator.com). They ranged from four to thirty-eight pages, with an average of eight pages each.

Day Six: Final Review

The final important follow-up was to revisit the question asked before we started the unit: *What can you tell me about women who served in World War II?* This time their answers were considerably different.

Pre-Unit	Post-Unit
I don't know any women who served in WWII.	Many women served in WWII, and many of them had different roles. You had women who were spies, like Virginia Hall, there were women who were snipers, like Lyudmila Pavlichenko, and there were women who worked the factory jobs. All of these roles were crucial in helping the Allies defeat the Axis in WWII. The women who served in WWII were really heroic. They helped inspire future women who wanted to serve in the military.
I can't name any specific women who served in WWII.	I have learned that women within WWII served various different roles in a wide range of occupations within the war. There were many women within the air forces, serving as admirable spies, and some famous for aiding their comrades on the battlefield as nurses. For me in particular I researched a Soviet bomber pilot, Nadezhda Popova. I learned that women risked their lives by flying over the battlefield. I've read that Nazi forces had feared Popova's units in particular. And that if a Nazi troop had shot down even just one of the Night Witches' planes they'd be given an award. And that's just because of how much the Nazis feared their bombings.
I can't name anyone who served for WWII whether it was a man or woman.	I can name a few women who served in World War II: Jane Kendeigh, Ruby Bradley, Nancy Harkness, and Susan Ahn. I have heard many amazing stories of women. Like the woman who walked a long way with a prosthetic leg. Just because we are women doesn't mean we can't do what men do.

After students finished creating their books, Scott asked them to complete a self-assessment using a rubric. He asked them to explain their rationale for each grade they gave themselves. This was a trick. What he really wanted to be able to do was to use their own criticism against them to build their confidence. They are much harder on themselves than Scott ever would be, so this gives him an opportunity to disagree with their harsh criticism and compliment their work!

Scott

There are many peer-review protocols, but I like this TAG protocol that was given to me by CUE member Brent Warner (@BrentGWarner), a community college professor in Orange County, California. For distance learning, I embed this in our class discussion board, so that students can read each other's comments.

TAG Feedback Sentence Starters	
T Tell something you liked…	I think your example was… I really enjoyed…because… Your work displays… The strongest part of your work was… It really touched my heart when… I could really connect with…
A Ask a question…	What are…? What do…? Should you…? Why is…? Why do…? Where is…? When does…? Did you consider…?
G Give a positive suggestion…	One suggestion would be… I think you should add… Don't forget to… Think about adding… I'm confused by… You might want to change… One problem I see… I strongly suggest… One minor mistake… If you…it might…

Adam

It is essential to have students read and review each other's work. This ensures that each student's creative efforts are acknowledged and validated by multiple peers.

One of the best features of using EduProtocols as the basis for a project is that it requires students to present their work each day. Scott found that this was a high point of using EduProtocols during distance learning. Scott was able to hear from each student each day. Not only did the students get feedback from him, but they also got comments from their classmates in the online chat. Another benefit of hearing from each student each day is that it allowed Scott to identify students who had fallen behind and then schedule private conversations with them in order to coach them back up.

Racking and Stacking with Adam:

Smashing Sequence:
Fast and Curious – Frayer Model – 8 p*ARTS

Sequencing EduProtocols together in a Rack and Stack sequence to create a learning succession helps Adam's students move through the content of social studies quickly and with a very high level of success. In his middle school class, he likes to sequence EduProtocols together as students work toward a larger project, for example, in a lesson about the Magna Carta.

Students have very little background knowledge of the Magna Carta. To a seventh grader, the Magna Carta is an abstract idea, but it's an important concept that is built upon in eighth-grade government lessons. This Magna Carta lesson is a small part of a larger unit Adam uses to teach the Middle Ages. The students take on the role of medieval characters they create and go on eight different quests. The goal at the end of each quest is to have the students write a blog post from their character's perspective about different events from the Middle Ages.

Protocol One: Fast and Curious for Background Knowledge and Feedback

In this particular quest, the students learned about the Magna Carta, but the students lacked necessary background knowledge. This lack of knowledge shows when the Quizizz class average is low. Quizizz is great at letting Adam know the commonly missed questions and allows him to give effective feedback. The key here is to give the kids the quiz BEFORE the lesson.

Adam
It's crucial to give feedback immediately after the fi rst rep of Fast and Curious.

Protocol Two: Frayer Model for Background Knowledge

Adam then used the results of Fast and Curious to steer the class into a Frayer model with the words *Magna Carta*. With the Frayer, students created their definition for the Magna Carta and discovered that *Magna Carta* was Latin for *Great Charter*. Under Characteristics, he encouraged students to include four or more facts about people, places, and dates with the Magna Carta. They collected information such as King John, Runnymede, 1215, and limited government. Under the Examples heading, students listed documents influenced by the Magna Carta, such as the Constitution and Bill of Rights, two documents eighth graders focus on. Finally, for Non-examples, students listed unlimited government and used terms we studied earlier in the year such as monarchies and tyrannies. The idea behind using the Frayer model at the beginning of the sequence is to expose students to vital information before they go more in depth with a reading.

Adam

The images below and the Fast and Curious above tell the story of the Magna Carta as developed through our Rack and Stack.

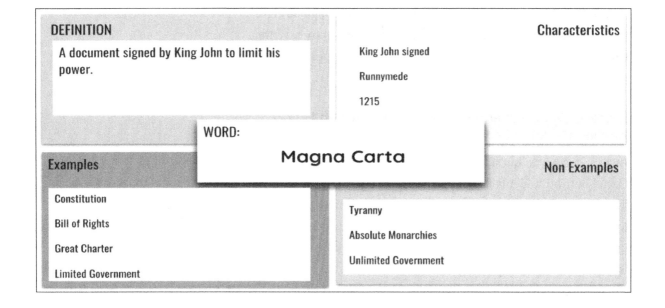

Protocol Three: Cyber Sandwich

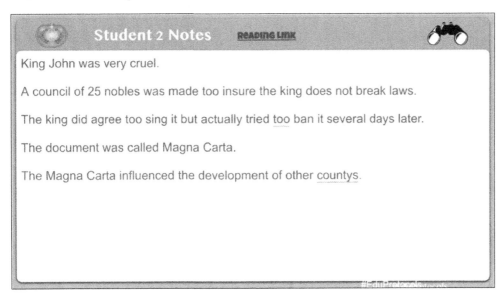

Student 2 Notes   READING LINK

King John was very cruel.

A council of 25 nobles was made too insure the king does not break laws.

The king did agree too sing it but actually tried too ban it several days later.

The document was called Magna Carta.

The Magna Carta influenced the development of other countys.

Once we established good background knowledge with the Frayer, students partnered up for a Cyber Sandwich. For ten minutes, students completed a one-page reading on the Magna Carta's history and influences. Then Adam encouraged them to take down five or more important facts. Students then discussed for five minutes, comparing notes about the Magna Carta. Finally, students took ten minutes to write a summary of the Magna Carta.

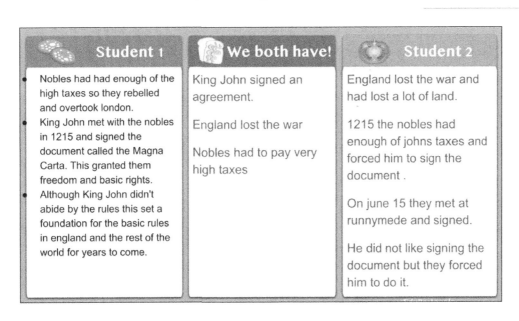

Student 1	**We both have!**	**Student 2**
• Nobles had had enough of the high taxes so they rebelled and overtook london. • King John met with the nobles in 1215 and signed the document called the Magna Carta. This granted them freedom and basic rights. • Although King John didn't abide by the rules this set a foundation for the basic rules in england and the rest of the world for years to come.	King John signed an agreement. England lost the war Nobles had to pay very high taxes	England lost the war and had lost a lot of land. 1215 the nobles had enough of johns taxes and forced him to sign the document . On june 15 they met at runnymede and signed. He did not like signing the document but they forced him to do it.

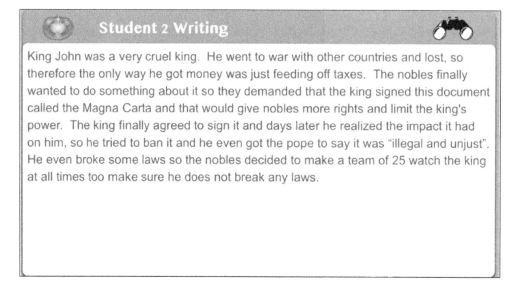

Student 2 Writing

King John was a very cruel king. He went to war with other countries and lost, so therefore the only way he got money was just feeding off taxes. The nobles finally wanted to do something about it so they demanded that the king signed this document called the Magna Carta and that would give nobles more rights and limit the king's power. The king finally agreed to sign it and days later he realized the impact it had on him, so he tried to ban it and he even got the pope to say it was "illegal and unjust". He even broke some laws so the nobles decided to make a team of 25 watch the king at all times too make sure he does not break any laws.

Protocol Four: Fast and Curious Second Round

Once the Cyber Sandwich concluded, students retook Fast and Curious Quizizz and raised their class average score.

Protocol Five: 8 p*ARTS

The ultimate goal of the Magna Carta lesson was to get students thinking from the perspective of their character about their feelings toward the Magna Carta. To get students thinking from a different point of view, Adam used 8 p*ARTS with a classic image of the Magna Carta signing. Students can make simple observations with nouns and verbs and use adjectives and adverbs to think from different perspectives. For example, they might say that King John was "angrily signing" or nobles were "cheerfully observing." (This is a wonderful scaffold for vocabulary development and also for ELL students.)

Three Word Title

pivot	in	history

Verbs	Adverbs	Summarize	Nouns	Adjectives
signing	forcibly	The year was 1215, and there was a pivot in history. With the death of Richard the Lionheart, his brother king john took over the throne. Like an unskippable ad, King John was disliked by everyone. It didn't take long for the displeased nobleman to hastily overthrow him, and waited patiently for him to sign the magna carta. They met King John in a green pasture in Runnymede in hopes of limiting his power.	pasture	green
waited	patiently		noblemen	despised
overthrow	hastily		King john	displeased

Time Period	Conjunctions
1215 - middle ages	and for but

Setting	Pronouns
Runnymede england	Them she he

Simile
Like an unskippable ad, he was disliked by everyone

Three Word Title

pivot	in	history

Verbs	Adverbs	Summarize	Nouns	Adjectives
signing	forcibly	The year was 1215, and there was a pivot in history. With the death of Richard the Lionheart, his brother king john took over the throne. Like an unskippable ad, King John was disliked by everyone. It didn't take long for the displeased nobleman to hastily overthrow him, and waited patiently for him to sign the magna carta. They met King John in a green pasture in Runnymede in hopes of limiting his power.	pasture	green
waited	patiently		noblemen	despised
overthrow	hastily		King john	displeased

Time Period	Conjunctions
1215 - middle ages	and for but

Setting	Pronouns
Runnymede england	Them she he

Simile
Like an unskippable ad, he was disliked by everyone

Final Product

Racking and stacking these EduProtocols together helped students understand the Magna Carta from multiple perspectives. The Fast and Curious protocol is a quick way to expose students to what they will be learning and receive immediate feedback on their responses. The Frayer model is a simple organizer for facts and a class discussion. The Cyber Sandwich allows students to create non-example notes of important facts, have discussions, and summarize the Magna Carta. The 8 p*ARTS EduProtocol helps the students think about an event from different perspectives and summarize their learning from day one of our lesson.

Magna Carta

Some kings throughout the kingdom have ruled very harshly. God mostly put them in power, therefore, they feel as if they can do whatever they want. However, as a Noble, I am rising up and wanting to make changes here.

I would like to have rights too. King John is abusing his power and he is starting to raise up our taxes. If my family doesn't pay the rent, then we get put in the jail. Because of this, they created the Magna Carta.

This document is very important to my fellow nobles because it gives us rights that King John wanted to take away. The Magna Carta increased the power for us because we finally had said something to King John. He was starting to be very mean, well he has always been like that. I took our rights away and my friend Esteban, and his family got taken away and now they are on their way back to Jerusalem. We have stayed in touch by writing letters back and forth. The Magna Carta limits the kings power because a king's decision has to pass through first.

Being creative with EduProtocol Rack and Stack sequencing can supercharge your students' learning. Remember, when we spend time at the beginning of the year introducing these protocols in a quick, fun way, building culture and establishing learning routines, we can go faster and get through more content later on. Sequencing can help create a seamless protocol transition from class to class and allows you to draw on multiple protocols to strengthen retention.

Teacher Big Ideas:

Marlena
Go slow to go fast!. Time and effort in training up students will pay off sooner than you realize!

Helping our students build background knowledge at various levels is important for any subject. When students have background knowledge, it helps us as teachers create more engaging questions, projects, and assessments. Racking and stacking EduProtocols is a great way to engage students throughout the learning process for an entire lesson or unit.

For some students, sequencing in a Rack and Stack helps overcome executive function deficits that prevent them from completing large projects. Many students finish several components of a project but never turn it in because they haven't completed every part, and they think they will get a low grade. We have found that when we stack EduProtocols, students complete every component of the project in class and are more likely to turn the project in, even if it hasn't been finished to their standards of perfection.

ELL Tips:

Listening activities help students improve their pronunciation, grow their vocabulary, and increase their English comprehension. Including audiobooks helps ELL students understand complex texts. Starting class with a listening exercise is a great way to get them warmed up for social studies content. Asking students to listen to part of a story and then retell it by smashing a Sketch and Tell with a Retell in Rhyme or Archetype Four Square gets your students practicing with academic language.

Conclusion

"**How will we know when we are done?**" Adam asked this question at the beginning of our collaboration on this book. We didn't know it at the time, but the answer was "When we run out of time and space." We could keep talking, improving, and collaborating for at least three more books, or possibly forever. We have delighted in sharing and celebrating the work of our students, tapped each other's expertise when designing new EduProtocols experiences, but most importantly, we have had extensive conversations about how to become better teachers.

Working with Jon and Marlena has taught us that sometimes the most productive collaborations are those that take place across school sites. The good news is that all teachers can have this experience. Collaborating within the #EduProtocol community is easy, whether you are on Twitter, Instagram, or at your brick-and-mortar school site. There's no need to start your EduProtocol journey alone. Reach out to someone who shares work you like on social media and make a new friend. You might be surprised where it takes you.

Because EduProtocols provide our students with familiar frames, we can space our lessons, slip in more retrieval practice, and improve reflective or metacognitive skills. The familiarity of EduProtocols also allows teachers to avoid cognitive overload and enables students to get more practice with the concepts and skills they have learned. EduProtocols make it easier for teachers to present social studies content in small steps. The collaborative aspect of

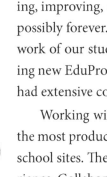

Scott

I never knew it was possible for me to feel this way about a vegetarian.

learning with EduProtocols ensures students see more exemplars. When this is combined with consistent and positive feedback in debriefing or coaching sessions, EduProtocols put students on the path to a growth mindset. Over time, students understand all the steps necessary in completing complex tasks, and they will be less likely to be sidetracked by task-initiation obstacles, small errors, or just good, old-fashioned teenage procrastination.

Too often we see great ideas online or learn techniques from books for our classrooms and feel there's only one way to implement these ideas. The great thing about EduProtocols is that you can adapt them to the needs of your students and think outside of the box. EduProtocols can be used creatively in a number of different ways, across grade levels and subjects. In this book, we've looked at EduProtocols through a social studies lens and adapted them for the needs of our students and lessons. We hope this work helps you bring more variety and depth of learning to your instruction.

We now invite you to join us in the conversation.

Acknowledgments

From Adam: I don't know why, but as an undergrad student at Northern Kentucky University, I dreamed of writing a book. This dream is now a reality, and I want to thank the following people:

Thank you to my wife, Stephanie, and two awesome daughters, Lennon and Teddy. Your support and understanding allowed this book to happen. Thank you to Jon Corippo and Marlena Hebern for taking a chance on me and changing my education career. Thank you to Dave and Shelley Burgess for making this book possible. I'm excited to be a part of the DBC family. Thank you to all the teachers who I collaborate with through Twitter and other social media platforms. You are truly an inspiration and I love learning from all of you.

From Scott: I first met Jon Corippo on a WWII aircraft carrier. The USS Hornet was awarded nine Battle Stars for its service in the Pacific. She saw action in historic battles at Leyte Gulf, Okinawa, and Iwo Jima. In a mere eighteen months of combat, her crew shot down 668 Japanese planes at sea and destroyed another 742 planes on the ground. She sank 73 ships and damaged another 413. This was a hallowed ground for history teachers. Jon arranged a weekend workshop where we got to spend a night on the ship and live like WWII sailors. For two days, we learned from top-notch teachers in ready rooms where real pilots had prepped for their missions. The experience exemplified the power of place-based learning. It was immersive, inspiring, and incredible. I wish all social studies educators could experience this type of inspiration. Please join your local affiliate of the National Council for the Social Studies or your state council and create the professional development necessary to advance our field. Learning from teachers is the best way to learn. Thank you, Jon, for introducing me to the EduProtocols squad. Thanks to my wife Sheila and daughters Sarah and Sam for giving me enough alone time to put these words on paper. Thank you to Adam, Marlena, Lindsey, and the Dave Burgess team for making me seem smarter than I really am.

Continue the Journey

The EduProtocol Field Guide, Book 1
by Marlena Hebern and Jon Corippo

The original sixteen EduProtocols are explained in this book with directions and tips for success. This book also contains the story of Tommy, guidelines for Smart Start, building culture in a classroom, and recalibrating creativity with the Four Cs Throwdown. (Note: The math-specific protocols from this book, Learning in the Round, and 3-Act Math® were reprinted in *The EduProtocol Field Guide: Math Edition*.)

The EduProtocol Field Guide, Book 2
by Marlena Hebern and Jon Corippo

An additional twelve EduProtocols are included in *The EduProtocol Field Guide, Book 2*, along with remixes inspired by readers using some of the original sixteen EduProtocols. Book 2 also contains insights into how instructional design theories underpin the protocols, stacking and smashing EduProtocols, and how the EduProtocols fit into the Universal Design for Learning classroom.

Deploying EduProtocols
by Kimberly Voge

Building on the instructional frames introduced in the EduProtocols Field Guides, Deploying EduProtocols premieres fun and effective new protocols and reveals how, when used strategically, these frames can help you teach more content for deeper learning and streamline your lesson planning–whether you're teaching in person or online.

The EduProtocol Field Guide, Math Edition
by Lisa Nowakowski and Jeremiah Ruesch

Thoughtfully and comprehensively presented with step-by-step instructions for implementation, each EduProtocol is designed with Common Core standards and Four Cs practices in mind. Whether you are new to EduProtocols or an experienced teacher looking to add even more tools to your pedagogical toolkit, The EduProtocol Field Guide: Math Edition has something for everyone interested in customizable student-centered learning activities.

Notes

Chapter 2: What Are EduProtocols

1. Partnership for 21st Century Skills, "P21 Common Core Toolkit: A Guide to Aligning the Common Core State Standards with the Framework for 21st Century Skills." (2011) files.eric.ed.gov/fulltext/ED543030.pdf P21.org
2. Anne Meyer, David Gordon, and David H. Rose, *Universal Design for Learning: Theory and Practice* (Wakefield, MA: CAST Professional Publishing, 2014).
3. L. S. Vygotsky, "Thinking and Speech." In R. W. Rieber and A. S. Carton (eds.)., *The Collected Works of L. S. Vygotsky, Vol. 1, Problems of General Psychology* (New York: Plenum Press, 1934), 39–288.

Chapter 3: Fast and Curious EduProtocol

1. Pooja K. Agarwal, Henry L. Roediger III, Mark A. McDaniel, and Kathleen McDermott, *Retrieval Practice Guide*. retrivalpractice.org. Retrieved December 23, 2021, from pdf.retrievalpractice.org/RetrievalPracticeGuide.pdf
2. Hermann Ebbinghaus, Urmanuskript "Über das Gedächtniß" (Passau: Passavia Universitätsverlag, 1880).
3. John Hattie, "Updated List of Factors Related to Student Achievement: 252 Influences and Effect Sizes," visible-learning.org/hattie-ranking-influences-effect-sizes-learning-achievement/.
4. Linda C. Hodges, Lisa C. Beall, Eric C. Anderson, Tara S. Carpenter, Lili Cui, Elizabeth Feeser, Tiffany Gierasch, Kalman M. Nanes, H. Mark Perks, and Cynthia Wagner, "Effect of Exam Wrappers on Student Achievement in Multiple, Large STEM Courses," *Journal of College Science Teaching* 50, no. 1 (2020): 69–79, jstor.org/stable/27119232.
5. Jaap M. J. Murre and Joeri Dros, "Replication and Analysis of Ebbinghaus' Forgetting Curve," *PLOS ONE* 10, no. 7 (2015), doi.org/10.1371/journal.pone.0120644.
6. Annie Paul Murphy, "Researchers Find That Frequent Tests Can Boost Learning," *Scientific American*, August 1, 2015. Retrieved December 23, 2021, from scientificamerican.com/article/researchers-find-that-frequent-tests-can-boost-learning/

Chapter 4: Thin Slides EduProtocol

1. Ignite Talks PBC. ignitetalks.io/
2. Cecil Stoughton, *Johnson Taking Oath*. Dallas, Texas, November 22, 1963. Photograph. loc.gov/item/00652311/.

Chapter 9: Frayer EduProtocol

1. Douglas Fisher, Nancy Frey, John Hattie, and Marisol Thayre, *Teaching Literacy in the Visible Learning Classroom: 6-12 Classroom Companion to Visible Learning for Literacy* (Thousand Oaks, CA: Corwin, 2017).

2. John Hattie, "Updated List of Factors Related to Student Achievement: 252 Influences and Effect Sizes," visible-learning.org/hattie-ranking-influences-effect-sizes-learning -achievement/.

3. John Hattie, Julie Stern, Douglas Fisher, and Nancy Frey, *Visible Learning for Social Studies, Grades K-12: Designing Student Learning for Conceptual Understanding* (Thousand Oaks, CA: Corwin, 2020), 48.

Chapter 10: Sketch and Tell EduProtocol

1. John Hattie, Julie Stern, Douglas Fisher, and Nancy Frey, *Visible Learning for Social Studies, Grades K-12: Designing Student Learning for Conceptual Understanding* (Thousand Oaks, CA: Corwin, 2020), 48.

Chapter 13: Archetype Four Square EduProtocol

1. Carol Booth Olson, Robin C. Scarcella, and Tina Matuchniak, *Helping English Learners to Write: Meeting Common Core Standards, Grades 6–12* (New York: Teachers College Press, 2014).

Chapter 14: Hero's Journey EduProtocol

1. Joseph Campbell, *The Hero with a Thousand Faces, vol. 17* (San Francisco: New World Library, 2008).

2. Carol Booth Olson, Robin C. Scarcella, and Tina Matuchniak, *Helping English Learners to Write: Meeting Common Core Standards, Grades 6–12* (New York: Teachers College Press, 2014).

3. Christopher Vogler, *The Writer's Journey* (Studio City, CA: Michael Wiese Productions, 2007).

Chapter 15: Retell in Rhyme EduProtocol

1. John Hattie, "Updated List of Factors Related to Student Achievement: 252 Influences and Effect Sizes," visible-learning.org/hattie-ranking-influences-effect-sizes-learning-achievement/.

2. Robert J. Marzano, *Building Background Knowledge for Academic Achievement: Research on What Works in Schools* (Alexandria, VA: ASCD, 2004).

Chapter 16: Research EduProtocol

1. Irene C. Fountas and Gay Su Pinnell, "Guided Reading: The Romance and the Reality," The Reading Teacher, 66, no. 4 (2012), 268–284.

About the Authors

Dr. Scott M. Petri has taught social studies at the middle and high school levels since 2003. He has also served as a coordinator and small school principal in LAUSD. He holds a doctorate in Educational Leadership and a Master's in Educational Administration from California State University Northridge and a BA in Political Science from the University of San Diego. Dr. Petri was named the 2021 Outstanding California Social Studies Teacher of the Year by the California Council for the Social Studies and has twice been a finalist for the CUE LeRoy's Big Idea contest.

Adam Moler has a passion for designing and creating lessons to engage all students. He continues to work at developing a student-centered classroom focused around critical thinking, creative thinking, collaboration, and communication, getting students more involved with learning history.

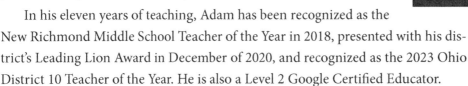

Adam loves to share his passion for great teaching and learning with other educators. His blog, Moler's Musings, shares his weekly reflections and thought process through lesson design. He has also presented in-person and virtually for teachers all over the world.

In his eleven years of teaching, Adam has been recognized as the New Richmond Middle School Teacher of the Year in 2018, presented with his district's Leading Lion Award in December of 2020, and recognized as the 2023 Ohio District 10 Teacher of the Year. He is also a Level 2 Google Certified Educator.

Before becoming an educator, Adam was a tennis instructor, tournament director, and tennis director at various clubs in Cincinnati, Ohio. The ideas of repetition and feedback through tennis instruction helped shape his educational philosophy. This is also a big reason EduProtocols resonated with him. He was drawn to the idea of letting students create their own learning with repetition and feedback in real time.

Adam is a graduate of Northern Kentucky University with a Bachelor of Arts in Integrated Social Studies, grades 7 through 12. He got his start in education as a paraprofessional in a social communication unit at Amelia High School. Upon leaving Amelia High School and switching to New Richmond Middle School, Adam obtained a Master of Science in Special Education from Western Governors University in 2014. Adam has been a teacher at New Richmond Middle School for the past ten years, teaching special education for two years and eighth grade social studies for the past eight years.

Adam lives in Cincinnati, Ohio (Who Dey!) with his wife, two daughters, and their tiny beagle.

For over thirty years, **Marlena Hebern** has been a passionate educator, putting her heart and soul into her work and loving every minute. Marlena is driven by kids and her desire to make learning fun and engaging for all students. Through her career as teacher, coach, administrator, and technology integration specialist, she has learned the value of relationships and supporting teachers.

Marlena Hebern's gentle and calm approach connects well with educators, especially those struggling to keep up. She draws upon her eighteen years of classroom experience, expertise with the EduProtocols, and Cognitive Coaching training to inspire and excite teachers about the possibilities of great instruction!

Marlena Hebern and her co-author were honored in 2020 as the recipients of the EdTech Awards in the category of Leader Setting a Trend. Marlena has also been recognized as a Beginning Teacher Support Provider of the Year and has a master's degree in Reading Instruction. She is also a Google Certified Innovator and a Google Certified Trainer. Marlena also presents at local and regional conferences including CUE and ISTE.

Marlena now lives in Maryland near her two daughters, sons-in-law, and grandchild. She enjoys exploring her surrounding community in beautiful Maryland.

Jon Corippo describes himself as a "formerly disgruntled student." He made it almost all the way through school at a 2.9 GPA. His final three semesters in advertising changed everything, though: advertising classes were project based. Jon's grades shot to nearly 4.0. Also while at Fresno State, Jon served as a graduate assistant football coach, learning about leadership and teaching at the feet of Jim Sweeney. Jon graduated college with no intention of teaching.

After about seven years in non-educational jobs, Jon's amazing wife persuaded him to try his hand in education: he was hooked after just two days as a long-term sub on an emergency credential.

About twenty years later, Jon had served a decade at the K–8 level, opened a 1-1, PBL, Google-based high school, served in two county offices, including as an Assistant Superintendent and IT Director. Jon has been recognized a County Teacher of the Year, a 20 to Watch Educator by the NSBA, a 100 to Watch Educator, and was a finalist and a winner in the EdTech Digest Awards for Eduprotocols. Jon also holds the Apple Distinguished Educator, Google Certified Innovator, and Microsoft Innovative Educator badges.

Jon is very proud of his work with CUE, where he served as the Chief Learning Officer. His work with CUE included creating the CUE Rock Star concept of Professional Development, with a focus on hands-on learning and getting teachers connected via social media. Jon led the development of the very successful CUE Google Launch program and the well received CUE BOLD Symposium. Under Jon's leadership, CUE professional learning trained over 50,000 educators.

In 2020–21, Jon returned to the classroom to reconnect with kids and update/create new EduProtocols. It was a trying time, in the middle of a pandemic, but Jon enjoyed his return to the classroom immensely.

Jon now supports the EduProtocols community full time, working with schools globally. Jon was able to do live classroom demos in over 180 classrooms in 2021–22.

Jon lives in Coarsegold, California, near Yosemite, with his wife (a very successful educator), three children, and a random number of free-range chickens.

More from

Dave Burgess Consulting, Inc.

Since 2012, DBCI has been publishing books that inspire and equip educators to be their best. For more information on our titles or to purchase bulk orders for your school, district, or book study, visit **DaveBurgessConsulting.com/DBCIbooks**.

Like a PIRATE™ Series

Teach Like a PIRATE by Dave Burgess
eXPlore Like a PIRATE by Michael Matera
Learn Like a PIRATE by Paul Solarz
Plan Like a PIRATE by Dawn M. Harris
Play Like a PIRATE by Quinn Rollins
Run Like a PIRATE by Adam Welcome
Tech Like a PIRATE by Matt Miller

Lead Like a PIRATE™ Series

Lead Like a PIRATE by Shelley Burgess and Beth Houf
Balance Like a PIRATE by Jessica Cabeen, Jessica Johnson, and Sarah Johnson
Lead beyond Your Title by Nili Bartley
Lead with Appreciation by Amber Teamann and Melinda Miller
Lead with Culture by Jay Billy
Lead with Instructional Rounds by Vicki Wilson
Lead with Literacy by Mandy Ellis
She Leads by Dr. Rachael George and Majalise W. Tolan

Leadership & School Culture

Beyond the Surface of Restorative Practices by Marisol Rerucha
Change the Narrative by Henry J. Turner and Kathy Lopes
Choosing to See by Pamela Seda and Kyndall Brown
Culturize by Jimmy Casas
Discipline Win by Andy Jacks
Escaping the School Leader's Dunk Tank by Rebecca Coda and Rick Jetter
Fight Song by Kim Bearden
From Teacher to Leader by Starr Sackstein

If the Dance Floor Is Empty, Change the Song by Joe Clark

The Innovator's Mindset by George Couros

It's OK to Say "They" by Christy Whittlesey

Kids Deserve It! by Todd Nesloney and Adam Welcome

Let Them Speak by Rebecca Coda and Rick Jetter

The Limitless School by Abe Hege and Adam Dovico

Live Your Excellence by Jimmy Casas

Next-Level Teaching by Jonathan Alsheimer

The Pepper Effect by Sean Gaillard

Principaled by Kate Barker, Kourtney Ferrua, and Rachael George

The Principled Principal by Jeffrey Zoul and Anthony McConnell

Relentless by Hamish Brewer

The Secret Solution by Todd Whitaker, Sam Miller, and Ryan Donlan

Start. Right. Now. by Todd Whitaker, Jeffrey Zoul, and Jimmy Casas

Stop. Right. Now. by Jimmy Casas and Jeffrey Zoul

Teachers Deserve It by Rae Hughart and Adam Welcome

Teach Your Class Off by CJ Reynolds

They Call Me "Mr. De" by Frank DeAngelis

Thrive through the Five by Jill M. Siler

Unmapped Potential by Julie Hasson and Missy Lennard

When Kids Lead by Todd Nesloney and Adam Dovico

Word Shift by Joy Kirr

Your School Rocks by Ryan McLane and Eric Lowe

Technology & Tools

50 Things to Go Further with Google Classroom by Alice Keeler and Libbi Miller

50 Things You Can Do with Google Classroom by Alice Keeler and Libbi Miller

140 Twitter Tips for Educators by Brad Currie, Billy Krakower, and Scott Rocco

Block Breaker by Brian Aspinall

Building Blocks for Tiny Techies by Jamila "Mia" Leonard

Code Breaker by Brian Aspinall

The Complete EdTech Coach by Katherine Goyette and Adam Juarez

Control Alt Achieve by Eric Curts

The Esports Education Playbook by Chris Aviles, Steve Isaacs, Christine Lion-Bailey, and Jesse Lubinsky

Google Apps for Littles by Christine Pinto and Alice Keeler

Master the Media by Julie Smith

Raising Digital Leaders by Jennifer Casa-Todd

Reality Bytes by Christine Lion-Bailey, Jesse Lubinsky, and Micah Shippee, PhD

Sail the 7 Cs with Microsoft Education by Becky Keene and Kathi Kersznowski

Shake Up Learning by Kasey Bell

Social LEADia by Jennifer Casa-Todd

Stepping Up to Google Classroom by Alice Keeler and Kimberly Mattina

Teaching Math with Google Apps by Alice Keeler and Diana Herrington

Teachingland by Amanda Fox and Mary Ellen Weeks

Teaching with Google Jamboard by Alice Keeler and Kimberly Mattina

Teaching Methods & Materials

All 4s and 5s by Andrew Sharos

Boredom Busters by Katie Powell

The Classroom Chef by John Stevens and Matt Vaudrey

The Collaborative Classroom by Trevor Muir

Copyrighteous by Diana Gill

CREATE by Bethany J. Petty

Deploying EduProtocols by Kim Voge, with Jon Corippo and Marlena Hebern

Ditch That Homework by Matt Miller and Alice Keeler

Ditch That Textbook by Matt Miller

Don't Ditch That Tech by Matt Miller, Nate Ridgway, and Angelia Ridgway

EDrenaline Rush by John Meehan

Educated by Design by Michael Cohen, The Tech Rabbi

The EduProtocol Field Guide by Marlena Hebern and Jon Corippo

The EduProtocol Field Guide: Book 2 by Marlena Hebern and Jon Corippo

The EduProtocol Field Guide: Math Edition by Lisa Nowakowski and Jeremiah Ruesch

Expedition Science by Becky Schnekser

Frustration Busters by Katie Powell

Fully Engaged by Michael Matera and John Meehan

Game On? Brain On! by Lindsay Portnoy, PhD

Guided Math AMPED by Reagan Tunstall

Innovating Play by Jessica LaBar-Twomy and Christine Pinto

Instructional Coaching Connection by Nathan Lang-Raad

Instant Relevance by Denis Sheeran

Keeping the Wonder by Jenna Copper, Ashley Bible, Abby Gross, and Staci Lamb

LAUNCH by John Spencer and A.J. Juliani

Make Learning MAGICAL by Tisha Richmond

Pass the Baton by Kathryn Finch and Theresa Hoover

Project-Based Learning Anywhere by Lori Elliott

Pure Genius by Don Wettrick

The Revolution by Darren Ellwein and Derek McCoy

Shift This! by Joy Kirr

Skyrocket Your Teacher Coaching by Michael Cary Sonbert

Spark Learning by Ramsey Musallam

Sparks in the Dark by Travis Crowder and Todd Nesloney

Table Talk Math by John Stevens

Unpack Your Impact by Naomi O'Brien and LaNesha Tabb

The Wild Card by Hope and Wade King

Writefully Empowered by Jacob Chastain

The Writing on the Classroom Wall by Steve Wyborney

You Are Poetry by Mike Johnston

Inspiration, Professional Growth & Personal Development

Be REAL by Tara Martin

Be the One for Kids by Ryan Sheehy

The Coach ADVenture by Amy Illingworth

Creatively Productive by Lisa Johnson

Educational Eye Exam by Alicia Ray

The EduNinja Mindset by Jennifer Burdis

Empower Our Girls by Lynmara Colón and Adam Welcome

Finding Lifelines by Andrew Grieve and Andrew Sharos

The Four O'Clock Faculty by Rich Czyz

How Much Water Do We Have? by Pete and Kris Nunweiler

P Is for Pirate by Dave and Shelley Burgess

A Passion for Kindness by Tamara Letter

The Path to Serendipity by Allyson Apsey

Rogue Leader by Rich Czyz

Sanctuaries by Dan Tricarico

Saving Sycamore by Molly B. Hudgens

The SECRET SAUCE by Rich Czyz

Shattering the Perfect Teacher Myth by Aaron Hogan

Stories from Webb by Todd Nesloney

Talk to Me by Kim Bearden

Teach Better by Chad Ostrowski, Tiffany Ott, Rae Hughart, and Jeff Gargas

Teach Me, Teacher by Jacob Chastain

Teach, Play, Learn! by Adam Peterson

The Teachers of Oz by Herbie Raad and Nathan Lang-Raad

TeamMakers by Laura Robb and Evan Robb

Through the Lens of Serendipity by Allyson Apsey

The Zen Teacher by Dan Tricarico

Children's Books

Beyond Us by Aaron Polansky

Cannonball In by Tara Martin

Dolphins in Trees by Aaron Polansky

I Can Achieve Anything by MoNique Waters

I Want to Be a Lot by Ashley Savage

Micah's Big Question by Naomi O'Brien

The Princes of Serendip by Allyson Apsey

Ride with Emilio by Richard Nares

The Wild Card Kids by Hope and Wade King

Zom-Be a Design Thinker by Amanda Fox

Made in the USA
Monee, IL
30 August 2022

12867039R00083